I Believe in Miracles
because I am one.
Because there's no
doubt in my mind that
I am only here today
because of God's grace
and mercy.

FACE THE FIRE

THIRD EDITION

By

Michael Sinclair Walter

Published 2020

Amazon Publication

A

TRUE

STORY

To my Mother, my wife Kelley, my daughter's
Kyleigh and Anie Thank you from the bottom of my
heart, for all the work and long hours you all put in
this book. Also in helping me get my life together and
my story out and told. In the hopes that it might help
someone else, like you all have help me

Dedication to my GOD

To my mother, for her courage and strength during her battle with cancer. To my father, for tolerating and understanding the wild side in me. To my two sisters, Donna and Karen, for their love and support over the years. To my brother, Rick, for his endless help in bringing this book to life. To the most important lady in my life my daughter, Kyleigh, This book is all for you in the hope that one day, you will come to understand my life and why your Father did the things he did, why things happened the way they did, and that one day, I will be able to see you again. To all my running brothers, you know who you are—I love you all. To all the stuntmen and stuntwomen who are here and still able to work in this wonderful yet hard-to-understand busi ness, and to those who have gone home. **Special thanks to the Redondo Beach CA, Fire Dept Station 2, on Grant Street**. Who on May 22nd 1980 at mid-night would saved my life. To all the producers, directors, cast and crews I have worked with overthe years— there will always be a special place in my heart for you all.

In the year of our Lord 2006, on November 23 rd, it was a Thanksgiving night, at 8:40 p.m. my best friend in the whole wide world lose her battle with lung cancer. In many ways, she was the strongest person I have ever met. She taught me many lessons in life, about people, and friendship, about love and family. What I witnessed that night I do not wish upon a single soul. Jeanne Marie Walter died in my arms and in the arms of my brother and sisters. Mom, we all love you and will miss you for-ever.

JEANNE M. WALTER

October 11, 1927 - November 23, 2006

Mom and Dad on their 50th anniversary

MY FATHER, MOTHER, AND MICHAEL - 2004

KYLEIGH AND MICHAEL - 2003

A MOTHER'S LOVE

A mother's Love
Holds you in her arms
Smiles back at you
Brings laughter and joy
Listens carefully
Cares deeply
Speaks truthfully Teaches rightly
Moves Mountains
Strong as a lioness
Gentle as a lamb
Points the way to God

A mother's Love
Watches and waits
Holds you in her arms
Smiles back at you
Welcomes you home

~A.L. Smith

Table of Contents

Author's Note

Before beginning the third edition, I would like to explain something about the printing of the first and second editions. In the first edition, there are many typos and run-on sentences. The story line didn't flow and at times, it seemed confusing. In the second edition it was a much cleaner edited version, however, I want to explain that it was a very difficult time in my life, with the death of my mother and the legal troubles I had gotten myself into. Now, thirteen years later, much has changed in the world, my life, and in the story, so I thought I would have the book edit again and add some very important details. I moved away from Maryland out to the beautiful high desert state of New Mexico. That change brought its very own set of challenges to my life, but overall, it has become the best decision I have made in a long, long time. I have gotten back to living a life and to be walking with God. I do not wear a halo by any means, but I'm doing the best I can to live a Christian life. I have fallen in love with a great woman who has helped me "see the light" so to speak. She accepted me for who I was in the first place. Because of her unselfish attitude in life and all she does on a daily basis, it was not hard to realize how many more changes and growth I needed in my own life. We attend the same church and I have met her friends and her family, who accept me for not only what I was, but also who I am becoming. When my mom died, I was so lost. I ran away from the East coast, my family and friends. However, this time, without my even knowing it, I was running *to* something, not away from something.

FOREWORD

I initially met Mike Walter in 1974 when I opened the Kali Academy in Torrance, California. Mike was a young, talented, and enthusiastic martial artist. His promising martial arts career was interrupted when tragedy struck. Mike was injured in a horrific car accident. Nearly crippled for life, his return to the martial arts and his career as a professional stuntman is a moving and inspirational story—one of a man's indomitable spirit, courage, and unrelenting zest for life. Mike's determination in the face of adversity will inspire all.

Dan Inosanto, Founder/Head Instructor

Inosanto Academy of Martial Arts

Marina Del Rey, California, USA

With Danny Inosanto and friends at he 2005 Maryland National Martial Arts Tournament, Michael Walter came in 2nd place in the heavyweight division, Full contact stick fighting.

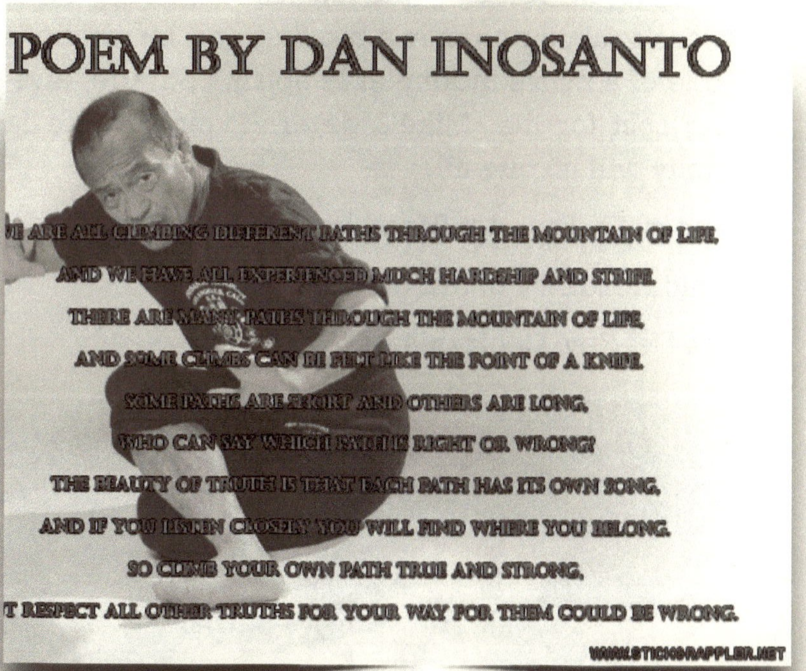
POEM BY DAN INOSANTO
E ARE ALL CLIMBING DIFFERENT PATHS THROUGH THE MOUNTAIN OF LIFE,
AND WE HAVE ALL EXPERIENCED MUCH HARDSHIP AND STRIFE.
THERE ARE MANY PATHS THROUGH THE MOUNTAIN OF LIFE,
AND SOME CLIMBS CAN BE FELT LIKE THE POINT OF A KNIFE.
SOME PATHS ARE SHORT AND OTHERS ARE LONG,
WHO CAN SAY WHICH PATH IS RIGHT OR WRONG?
THE BEAUTY OF TRUTH IS THAT EACH PATH HAS ITS OWN SONG,
AND IF YOU LISTEN CLOSELY YOU WILL FIND WHERE YOU BELONG.
SO CLIMB YOUR OWN PATH TRUE AND STRONG,
T RESPECT ALL OTHER TRUTHS FOR YOUR WAY FOR THEM COULD BE WRONG.
WWW.STICKGRAPPLER.NET

TESTIMONIALS

"It has been a pleasure working with Mike Walter because he is a top professional who gives me what I ask for in the safest possible way. He has developed a keen knowledge of camera and editing, which makes my job much easier. Many times, he has been able to come up with production ideas that have saved the production time and money and have actually enhanced production value. As a producer and director, I would use no one else."

~~ Mark Headley, Producer/Director

"The stunt work was precise and right on the money. I was very impressed by the way you put it all together for us. The high fall looked terrific, and we got it on all three cameras, you were great as an actor as well. Thanks again for being our stunt coordinator—you did an excellent job. I look forward to working with you again in the near future."

~~ Alec Griffith, Producer

"Mike Walter has done a project for my company as a stunt coordinator and stuntman. His skill and professional attitude was beneficial to the whole project. He is likable and a joy to work with."

~~ Norman Vane, Producer/Director

"Mike is amazing! He was once confined to a wheelchair, yet he's now able to do the most difficult stunts known to man."

~~ John Hagner, President, Hollywood Stuntman Hall of Fame

John Hagner had Mike's footprints preserved at the Hall for posterity.

"Clearly, making our film would have been impossible without a professional stunt team. Your services as stunt coordinator, as well as the talent of the stunt artists, where a wonderful asset to us and a great asset to Central Florida. "

~~ Ralph R. Clemente, Producer/Director

"I've known Mike Walter for some time now. It's unique to meet someone whose life has been filled with so many different emotions. For someone like Mike to hang out with a state trooper is unheard of. We first met when we lived at Regatta Bay in Annapolis, Maryland. We had a lot of good times hanging out in the pool, the cookouts, the parties in Club-G and getting in trouble with the management.

I personally believe I've helped Mike 'see the light at the end of the tunnel' in certain circumstances. For example, he learned not to drink to excess, not to talk to women in a mean and disrespectful way, and to understand that friends will always be there.

One night, while break dancing in Griffin's (a nightclub in Annapolis), he tore his hamstring attempting to do a split. The next day, Mike called me and told me I was right and that he was done drinking. He was sober for nine months! I know it was hard on him and it was especially hard on me. His attitude

And looks changed — he grew his hair back out and he started talking to people with respect, particularly women.

At the end of the nine months, Mike moved away from Annapolis and moved to the rural country side of the eastern shore of Maryland, a quiet, subdued place where there was no opportunity to engage in previous behaviors. Mike was a real estate agent during this time, and because there was little to do, Mike found it a difficult place to live. He wasn't selling homes and there was no movie work coming his way. One day Mike said, "The hell with it" He called me up, and we went out to the local bar and had a few drinks. The next week, Mike started selling houses, movie producers started calling him for work, and he shaved his head again.

After being friends with Mike Walter, I have learned something very special from him. Never live your life the

way others want you to live it; just be real to yourself and others and people will like you for who you are."

~~ Chris Bath, - Maryland State Police...

Staff photo by Bob Jones

One man is treated while firefighters work to free another after an accident in Redondo Beach. It took 30 minutes to get him out.

2 men seriously hurt when speeding truck hits tree in Redondo Beach

A truck careened over the top of a hill in Redondo Beach early today and crashed broadside into a tree, seriously injuring two men.

The accident occurred about midnight in the 1900 block of 190th Street.

David G. Welch Jr., 27, of Redondo Beach, who owns the truck, may have been catapulted through a rear window onto the truck bed, police said. That's where they found him.

Welch is in stable condition at South Bay Hospital.

Firefighters and paramedics had to work for 30 minutes with power tools to cut Michael S. Walter, 26, of Torrance out of the passenger side of the shattered vehicle.

Walter is in critical condition at the same hospital.

Firefighters said one of Walter's ankles was broken and wedged under the collapsed dashboard. Rescuers had to cut away the roof of the vehicle and pry the dashboard up to free him.

Police said an officer in a patrol car had spotted the truck moving fast on 190th Street just before the accident and was trying to catch up with it when it disappeared over the top of the hill at Flagler Lane.

Police said skid marks indicate the truck slid across westbound lanes, hit the 50-foot palm and spun 180 degrees.

1980

SAINT SIMONS ISLAND

Michael Sinclair Walter

37 years' experience in the fitness business.

Certified Martial Arts Master.

Former bodyguard for actor Lou Gossett Jr, singer Dave Mason,

Melissa Manchester, and Guru to the Beatles Maharishi

Former five-time world record holder on total fire engulfment

using Gary Zeller - Zel Gel

1993 Inducted into, Hollywood Stunt man Hall of Fame

12-year competitor in karate tournaments, boxing, and full-contact

martial arts demo's and tournaments

1973 – Competed in National Karate Association Grand National

1977 – Competed AKA Karate Olympics

1980 – Olympic Middleweight Boxing Contender: AAU Golden

Gloves, Diamond Belt Contender

1998 – Competed in the Gold Gym Classic

1998 – Competed in Gold Gym's "Mr. Wilmington".
1999 - Appeared on national TV's "Guinness Book of World Records"

2002 – Personal Fitness Trainer, I.F.P.A. Certified

2002 – 25 years in the entertainment industry as actor, stunt-man, stunt coordinator.

Member S.A.G., D.G.A., and I.F.P.A.

2005 – Second Place, Heavyweight Division, Maryland Nationals, full contact stick   fighting 2007 – Relocated to Albu-querque, NM

2008 – Served on Screen Actors Guild

National Stunt Safety Committee

For complete resume, search, Michael Sinclair Walter at https://
pro.imdb.com/name/nm0910095?ref_=hm_prof_name

THE MOST RIDICULOUS THING I'VE EVER HEARD

Street Fighting Championships

Oakland, California

His arm was wrapped around a neck

And pressing on another limb

Could not conceal troubled eyes so black

And so inflicted the pain with pain

A sound no ape would care to hear

Explode deep within his ear

He so was pinched by his neckless foe

That just his instincts let him go

Prone and pale his heart devoured

But never would he dare have cowered

So in-firmed for weeks he'd be

That no one else this wreck would see

Until all healed at last he'd stand

And pray again for the upper hand

And pray be gone the swollen eye

Next, let me win, or let me die

R. Walter - December 26, 1978

CHAPTER ONE: IN THE BEGINNING

My name is Michael Walter, and for much of my adult life, I was a professional Hollywood stuntman. To start this story off in the best way I know how is to explain that on May 22, 1980, I was involved in a high-speed police chase through the streets of Hermosa and Redondo Beach, California. Going at speeds close to 90 miles per hour. That chase ended in a terrible crash, and I died. I will provide more detail later, but first, I need to explain the story of where I am today. Because of my life experiences, I sometimes get confused at the timeline of my life, and since I am writing this story as though I were sitting down talking to you in person, I may jump around a bit as events come to mind. I believe it is important to explain that I am not doing this on purpose; at times, I forget certain things or certain events that have happened because of the injuries I have suffered. I will take you on my journey as I remember it, and maybe it will bring a memory of your own to mind or bring a smile to your face. Maybe it will also encourage you to sit yourself down and write your own story because everybody has one of their own. Years after experiencing a horrific car crash in 1980, I began writing a screenplay. I needed to tell my true feelings and the whole story of what happened to me, why my life ended up the way it did. The screenplay is finished, but so much more had to be told. I decided to write this book, I started this book when I was 53 years old, Now I am 66 years old, better late then never. I guess the best way to start this is at the beginning, or at least as far back as I can remember. As many know or those who have researched know, the 1960s were a challenging time in history, and I have great memories of that time. What I have discovered though in my short time here on planet earth is that we remember the good things that happen, which seem to balance life out with its share of bad things. Such is life, some things are just too painful to recall, or maybe I feel I just cannot share them with you at this point. I promise that as I tell you my story, you'll become acquainted with who I am, and I believe you will begin to understand why I did the things I did. I will be wearing my heart on my sleeve in the hope that what I have to say might help someone. There will be moments that might make you a little teary, and moments that may get you upset, but I promise you this—although the ending may not be what you hoped for or expected, it is still the real ending. It is not a make-believe or an "I wish" type of ending. It is simply the true story of my life. As I sit in my office in a rural farming town in the beautiful state of Maryland beginning to write my story, I cannot help but think about my childhood. I was born in Bethesda, Maryland on November 16, 1953. I am the youngest of four children, with one older brother and two older sisters. My father was an insurance executive, and my mother was a homemaker. My story begins where things are clearest to me, in 1961. My dad had gotten a new job in Dallas, Texas and we were off on a three-day drive. It seemed to me that everyone in my family was excited and happy about the move, something that happened a lot in our family as you will see. To properly set your perspective, classmates at my age and older students used to love to push me around, beat me up, and steal my lunch money. I do not want a pity-party, I am sure similar things like this happen in most people's lives as they grow up. Anyway, I did what most eight year-old boys do—I climbed trees and fell from those trees. I played in the woods with matches and accidentally set things on fire.

Fire–wow! I could write a whole chapter on this subject. I was drawn to the effects of fire—the heat, the color, the pain, and the wonder. It is really a beautiful thing to look at.

We lived in Texas for five years. Even though I was bullied, I still had fun times with friends back when I was a kid, though the enjoyment seems to differ from the days of pleasure and enjoyment now; times are sure changing. Kids at my age liked to play outside, go down to the local area creeks, go to pools, walk in the woods, and play football with no pads. They built go-karts, rode mini bikes, had family get-togethers, picnics, and caught fireflies. It was a pleasure just to be alive and really live life. Towns would put on large 4th of July events. Times were sure different. It seemed like a more pleasant, simpler time, and I miss those days. Today, the world just seems like it is headed down the wrong road. I was attending a Catholic school in Dallas on a normal day. The weather outside was pretty, and there was really nothing that would have led me to believe that the events which were about to happen on this day would change my life forever. Some say it was the day I lost my innocence; others say it was the day I went crazy.

I believe it was late morning, though I am not sure which day of the week it was. I was in the boy's bathroom when two other boys came in and started pushing me around. I tried to hold my own but they were too strong. I began to cry because I thought I knew what was about to happen; only this time, I was wrong. The two boys pushed and pulled me into the bathroom stall, as I yelled for them to stop, but to no avail. One boy grabbed me and put my head into the toilet; the other boy laughed and flushed the toilet so that the toilet water was going down my mouth and up my nose. I did manage to scream for help, and a priest walking in the hall heard me. He was a friend of my parents. He came running into the bathroom and broke it up. He sent the two boys who were beating on me to the head nun's office. They left and the priest stayed with me in the bathroom stall, helping to dry me off. He began to comfort me and to tell me that everything would be all right, and he promised me that I would feel better in a few minutes, then he said,"Michael, you have to promise me you will never tell anybody about this and keep this our secret." I said, "I know, Father, because if I tell, I will be sent to hell because I broke a promise to a Catholic priest." He told me that was correct and he closed the stall door, took off my pants, and started. Now, I know you are bright people and you can figure out what he started. Pretty messed up huh? Trust me; life did not get any better.

That night at home with my whole family, everybody was discussing how their day went as I stayed silent and drifted in thought. I was angry but too scared to tell anyone what had happened to me that day. It happened again later that year, but I did not tell anyone for twenty-two years. Think I had some issues? At a very young point in my life, I wanted to get out of my head, to have a different sense of reality, even though it was false. To accomplish this, I built model cars, planes and boats, which is where I found out what the effect of sniffing glue would have on me.

****

I made a mental note that the day I am starting to write this story is the five-year anniversary of September 11, 2001, the day America changed. It is a very emotional day of memories.

****

In 1967, once again, my family was moving. I guess it was for my Dad. It must have been a better job. For me, the moves started to become more difficult because I was getting older and I had friends and girlfriends. I did not have much say in whether we got to move, so we moved. This time, it was to Chicago, Illinois.

Actually, we lived in a suburb called Arlington Heights, an upper middle class area. At that age, I did not know that there were any social classes. I just thought people lived in homes, some better than others. At this time in my life, of course, my mother still bought my clothes. Looking back, I dressed rather fashionably, but to my classmates, well, they just nicknamed me Rainbow. With all this built up anger inside of me, I was fighting a lot and my parents were not too impressed. I was winning the fights, but I would come home with black eyes, cuts, and of course, the clothes they had just bought were torn or destroyed. I had so much anger that I got into a lot of trouble in school. Even so, I developed some close friendships that would also have an effect on my behavior and dealings with the law later in my life. Too bad I could not see into the future and change the course of my life back then. I was paying close attention to some people in the martial arts like Bruce Lee, Judo Gene LeBell, Chuck Norris, Bill Wallace, and of course, Alan Steen.

The following year, 1968, I started high school. I was now in a street gang and playing football. I tried the wrestling thing and gymnastics. I loved gymnastics and became pretty good at it. Trampoline and the rings were my specialty. On the morning of the gymnastics State Championships, I was practicing a double back flip, something not really done much in competition in those days. I was by myself and I had no safety belt on. I opened from the double back flip too soon. The landing caused me to crack my lower back. I did not pay attention to the injury until years later.

It was 1969, and I had been living in the Chicago area for two and a half years. At this point, I was older and did not want to move. I had developed deep friendships and had become a gymnastics star in my school. I was also in the leadership group of the street gang, All this was a big deal to me because before this time in my life, I was always in some sort of depression. Anyway conflicts began and continued with my family and police for some years to follow. My dad got a better job again and as always, I had no real say in the matter so off the family moved again to the eastern United States, to a country town in the state of Vermont. Talk about shock value! We had moved from an active mid-west city to a small cold mountain town. Montpelier, Vermont is the state Capitol, but oh my God! It was not my idea of where to live or even visit. In Vermont, the winter can last as long as four to five months. Some years, there are deep cold snowstorms, you need mental toughness to make it through those winters. Then again, it was one of the most enjoyable and beautiful places that I have ever lived. I learned to snow ski, drive snowmobiles, snowshoe, hike, and hunt deer and bears.

Picture this, me wearing a leather jacket, those pointed-toed shoes, a switchblade knife in my pocket next to all those hillbillies, lumberjacks, mountain men and women. Some of the biggest badass people I have ever met in my life, many of whom I learned to love and respect.

In this place, I learned to make a living for myself. My first job was in Chicago as a busboy in a restaurant at Randhurst Mall. My second job was in Vermont picking strawberries for about $1.50 a day, true story. I was still sixteen years old, and I remember it was going to be my second year in high school. That summer before school started, I met a lifeguard at the local pool, and I fell deeply in love with her. I allowed that relationship to cause more problems at home. Margie was the most wonderful girl I had ever met. I was still very shy towards females and she was a year ahead of me in school. I did not know it yet, but her father was my father's supervisor at National Life Insurance Co. I do not remember the timeline exactly, but I do remember it was a great summer. When school started, Margie and I became a real item. She drove since I did not have my driver's license, something I would be getting that fall. We would walk each other to classes, hang out in the library, have lunches together, and go out on dates.-I loved her so much. Margie was a cheerleader, and her male jock classmates did not like the idea of this street hood dating a cheerleader, so they let it be known. In groups they would try to mess with me. One night, I went to a party with Margie and her friends, we started drinking beer. I never drank before and got so drunk. That scene started a rollercoaster ride straight to hell for me. I am not blaming her, just stating the facts.

The following year, I began to hang out with less desirable elements in town—wrong people, wrong places. I started getting into trouble, doing jail time, getting speeding tickets, fighting, and drinking too much. That was Margie's senior year, and she was going away to college the following year. We both were getting pressure from our parents to cool the relationship, so we broke up and I started acting out more. I tried to join the Marine Corps because I wanted to go to Vietnam. Medical reasons kept me from not being able to join which was the final crushing blow to me. I was so angry deep inside, but I would not really know or understand just how much until years later. I had an older female friend who lived out in the country by my family's house. She was a nice girl who used to ride by my house on a chestnut horse. She drove a dark blue Mercury Cougar. Joanne was her name, and I had a major crush on her.

When Margie and I broke up, I turned to Joanne. However she was dating a guy named David, who drove a 1955 Chevy. Back then, muscle cars were the thing to drive. Then until around June of 1972, my life was full of troubles and conflict. My father and I butted heads about drinking, school grades, fights, the police, and haircuts. Joanne and I became closer friends. She would drive me around town, take me places, we would talk and laugh. Then another painful crushing blow came - Joanne would be getting married to her boyfriend. She invited me to the wedding and I went, but then I went home after the wedding and cried. It hurt a lot. As events in my life continued to mold my behavior, I was increasingly confused about why things happen the way they do in life.

By high school graduation, my parents and I were no longer talking. It was a very sad time, but I made a decision to move out of my parent's house a few weeks later. That would prove to be a huge mistake in my life, one that I can never take back. I can never forget the pain I caused my family for that move. I sold most of my belongings, including a shotgun my grandfather gave me and the car that my brother had given me. I hiked across the United States, up through Canada, for about a week. I stole a boat just outside Windsor, Canada to get across the Great Lakes into Chicago. Then I worked my way back out to Arlington Heights. For the next couple of years, I trained hard under the martial arts greats, Flem Evans and Kenny Knudsen.

I started getting into the drug scene, mostly LSD, POT, PCP, uppers and downers, and I was drinking a lot. God only knows why and how I lived through those years. I fought in the 1973 American Karate Association Grand

Nationals, but I was in and out of jail, in gang and bar fights. During that time, the gang I was involved in had street drag races. I drove a 1967 paneled Chevy van, with a Corvette engine (LT-1), tunnel ram, cheater slicks, racing transmission, and a straight axle front end. Everybody in the gang had to have a fast car or motorcycle. That was a big deal back then. I do not know if that stuff still happens today—it sure does not happen where I live now. We would race for pink slips, i.e., the title of the car, truck, or motorcycle. It was a wild time for me.

The area I lived in Arlington Heights, Illinois was known for having a bad cop or two; cops on the take, policemen giving beatings, things like that. Anyway, one night after a party, a friend and I got involved in a police chase. The police blocked us off and when we got out of the car, we got in a fist fight with the cops. After I punched out one of the cops, which by the way is not a real good idea, they arrested me and charged me with aggravated assault on a police officer. They kicked and beat me, breaking my jaw and ribs. *That was strike one.* After the trial I was released into my fathers custody, had to moved back to Vermont to my parents house. Then after probation, I moved to Dallas, Texas where my older sister Karen lived. I still kept getting into trouble.

Later that year, I fought in many karate tournaments, including the American Karate Association's Karate Olympics, held in Dallas. I lived in Dallas for a couple of years with my oldest sister Karen, then I got my own place. I would be accepted into the Los Angeles Boxing and Kali Academy. The instructors there were friends and training partners of the late Bruce Lee. I left Dallas in a beat-up Subaru car, said my goodbyes to my sister, and friends I had met there thanked her, and off I went. Moving around was just in my blood.

The drive out west was great. One night of the trip I stayed in a hotel in Arizona where I met and flirted with the female desk clerk. I had dinner with her that night, went to a movie, and off I went the next day. When I arrived in California, I fell in love with the state. I drove into to San Diego first and then up to Los Angeles. Back then, Kali Academy was in a suburb of Los Angeles called Torrance, Ca. When I finally got there, I had an interview with Richard Bustillo, one of the Academy owners and instructors. He told me that although I had over 12 years of martial arts experience, I would have to start in the beginner's class, which started the next month.

It was 1974, and the beaches were a safe place to party. As you will soon learn, I was one mixed up and confused young man with very deeply seated anger issues inside of me and no real understanding of how this anger was affecting my life. I believed that sex, drugs, and fighting were the answer and all I needed to make it in life. For a long time, that was true. I had some of the best times of my life in California and made some of my greatest friends there. However, there were also some of the most tragic and sad times in my life as well.

The following month, I started working as a plumber's helper to make a living. I trained at the Academy six days a week. For two days a week, I was doing a lot of drinking, cocaine, LSD, uppers, downers, heroin—anything to get me out of who I was, anything to prove to myself that I was a real man. In my mind, what happened to me as a child with that priest and what happened to me with those cops in Chicago always haunted me. I wanted those people to die. I had nightmares about them both. How could this happen to me? I trusted all those people. I was brought up to respect and believe, that figures like that stood up for what is right and wrong, not to do what they felt like if no one was looking.

Being messed up on drugs and alcohol worked for me for a long time. However, there were times I wished I could stop and just be normal, whatever "normal" was. I was so wrapped up in training, that I moved into a boarding house close to the Academy. I was living a double life with my training, and my drug addiction. You should know that in some instances, I will just elude to certain things to give the reader the understanding of what it is that I am actually talking about. I have to respect the rights of others and my family. Although they know most of the story, I have to show respect to them in the way I write this book and its content. I hope you will respect that and understand my reasons why I may seem vague sometimes in telling my story.

The Academy was like something right out of a *Kung Fu* TV series. As you walked into the school, there were weapons hanging on all four walls, heavy boxing bags, speed bags, mirrors, a concrete floor, pictures of Bruce Lee and other martial arts masters, a waiting area with chairs, couches, and of course, changing areas with two bathrooms. I trained on Monday, Wednesday and Saturdays at the Academy, and on my off days, I would teach others in my backyard or at someone else's house.

Chicago and California is where I began my work in the plumbing trade. At that point in my life, after working my way up from a helper, I became a journeyman plumber. I drove a plumbing truck and I had a helper, so my day would look like this: after working eight hours a day or longer, I would head home, shower and change, then head off to the Academy.

In 1974 I met Danny Inosanto and his business partner Richard Bustillo. It seemed at that time, that many people would come to train at the Academy in search of the Bruce Lee magic. I know it is not like that today in either one of

Danny's or Richard's schools, but back then, it seemed that way. I had been promoted several times over the years at the Academy, with my most recent promotion to the special JKD (Jeet Kune Do) class. We worked out in the dark sometimes, but the door was always locked. JKD had closed-door sessions, It was where the system that Bruce Lee created was taught, but even the name JKD bothered Mr. Lee, because he was just attempting to free individuals for self-expression, teaching them not to limit themselves to becoming a mechanical robot in the martial arts. Although Mr. Lee had passed away years before, his spirit was very much alive in the Academy, Bruce's family (wife, Linda and son, Brandon) often visited the school. I am not sure if I ever met his younger daughter, Shannon. We do share messages on Facebook sometimes though.

Up to this point in my life, I was torn between two worlds—the spiritual world and the world where I seemed locked in the late 1960s and early '70's. I was in search of my inner-self and peace, but always in conflict.

Reading both Zen and the Tao, and any book on the subjects of self enlightenment, I almost even became a Taoist monk at one point. On the other hand, I was also doing cocaine and any other drugs on the weekends. My relationship with my two martial arts instructors was growing very strong. I would have dinner with Danny sometimes after workouts, go on motorcycle rides with Richard on some weekends. I miss those days. I call them both every couple of years to say hello or send text now and then. (Richard has since passed away on March 30, 2017), during all this time. I never really had a steady girlfriend, I had a lot of one-night stands and many encounters with women, but I was much too busy training for the 1980 Olympics for a hopeful spot as a middleweight boxer. I used to do 1000 sit-ups and 1000 pushups a day. I was still working full-time. Sometimes I would run four to six miles a day, but I continued to use drugs and drink on the weekends. Over a ten year period, this behavior would result in eight car and motorcycle accidents.

Time was calling my number up, so to speak, however I didn't even realize it. I walked away from seven of those eight accidents. The one I did not walk away from would have a life changing effect on me, as well as my family and friends. In 1979, I was working full-time as a plumber, had a car, motorcycle, and house near the beach, and I was still in and out of the boxing ring, karate tournaments, also illegal underground fights, not yet popular the likes of (aka: fight club). I had a three weigh-in's for three more fights—I was training for, the Golden Gloves, Diamond Belt, then my try out for the 1980 Olympic Boxing team as a middleweight. However, I could not come down in weight. At that time, the middleweight class was in a range of 153-167 pounds, and I was at 172 pounds. My boxing coach, Mr. Art Saxell told me to train hard and we would pass the Olympics up and turn pro. The USA boycotted the Summer Olympic Games that year in Moscow anyway. The plan was to drop the weight and work my way up in rankings, to try and fight a middleweight fighter name Marvin Hagler. Mr. Hagler later became the middleweight champion of the

world. In life, if one does not find a balance in one's behavior, something will eventually break down. As that year wore on, I worked on a few films as an extra. I was training, partying, and working a lot more than I was used to.

In plumbing, there are times where one is on call twenty-four hours a day, I hated that. I would be sound asleep when the phone would ring. I would have to get up at 3:00 a.m. to drive across town to fix someone's toilet, shower or something that I thought could wait until the morning, but oh no, I had to get it fixed right then. I never did understand that. Now, getting up at 3:00 a.m. to work on a movie - now *that* was a different story. I would do that all the time if I could.

My party scene was rolling along as normal, So one weekend afternoon in May 1980, several of my friends and I had a big party down on beach at 2nd Street in Hermosa Beach, California. Everyone was drinking, swimming, doing drugs—back then, it was not a big deal. Today, you could never get away with what we used to get away with on the beach back then. The area consisted of the street that would end a few feet from the curb, then a walkway called the Strand, then a half wall, and then the beach. We used to park our cars on the street, our motorcycles on the Strand, and bicycles on the beach. We had been there all day with the sun beating down on us. Most of us were either drunk, stoned, coked (cocaine) out, speeding, all of the above, or passed out. Night was falling and I asked a friend of mine, Dave, to follow me home in his 1978 Ford Ranchero. We had no business on the road driving and endangering our lives and the lives of others, but we did just that. On the way, we picked up more beer, cocaine, and food for the party.

Off we roared like the two jerks we both were at the time. I guess that maybe a half hour went by. I lived very close and by then the stores had closed, so in no time, we were back at the party. It was late now, and everyone was messed up. It was a beautiful scene with the girls, the beach, the ocean, and a bonfire. As the night wore on, the more messed up every one became. People started to leave and the party started to break up. It was about 11:50 p.m. on May 22, 1980. It was time for me to go home too because I was to start a new plumbing job in the morning and start training for my next fight that evening. I had been seeing this a waitress for a while, but we had stopped dating a few weeks earlier. Her name was Jackie, and you will understand soon enough why I mention this.

Dave drove me home in his 1978 blue Ford Ranchero but there was just one problem. David was too messed up on beer and drugs to walk. So, as good friends do, I picked him up, carried him to the car, and put him in on the driver's side, of course I mean, it was his car. I got into the passenger side, we both did a line of cocaine, and off we drove. It was somewhere around 11:57pm. We sped through the streets of Hermosa and Redondo Beach, and turned left onto a street called 190th. As we turned the corner, a Redondo Beach police car started to pursue us. Dave and I decided to try to outrun the patrol car. The speed limit was 35 mph and we were already doing about 50 mph in Dave's Ford Ranchero, a

very fast car. He pushed the pedal to the floor as we traveled up 190th Street, and we now peaked the speed of the car at 90 mph.It's totally insane what and how I've learned things over the years. The first thing I learned is that you should never hit a cop, ever because he or she has thousands of brothers and sisters who carry guns and clubs, and you will never win. The second lesson I learned is that while you may think you have a fast car or motorcycle, you will never, ever outrun a police radio. Dave and I drove like a couple of insane men, singing, drinking, and running from the police. We would soon come to a complete stop.

Right at midnight, on May 22 nd 1980, Dave crossed an intersection at 190th Street and Flagler Lane on top of a hill. He lost control of the car and I of course, not being of sound mind thinking I was superman, was not wearing my seat belt. The next thing I remember is holding my arm in front of my face and lifting my right leg up straight out to protect me the best way I knew how. The car did a 180-degree spin and we crashed into

a 50-foot palm tree at 90 mph. Dave was thrown through the glass of the rear window onto the bed of the Ford Ranchero. I was not as lucky. We hit the palm tree on the passenger side of the vehicle and suddenly, I was no longer sitting in the original place I had been a few minutes earlier. Although I thought I was superman, I was wrong.

I told you this would get worse! You may think *strike two*. Nah! Close, but not yet. I was wedged in one square foot of twisted metal that wrapped around my body, bleeding profusely through my eyes, ears and legs. There was blood all around me, I would be told later. My eyes were wide open as I tried to pull myself out of the car with the only part of my body I could even move, which was my pinky finger on my right hand. Then in an instant, though no one yet knew it, I had slipped into a coma. Why was I moving, and why were my eyes open? There is a name for what was happening to me. I had slipped into a death coma with doll's eyes.

MICHAEL WALTER, FAMOUS AXE KICK

MICHAEL WALTER HIGH ROUND KICK - 1976

**MICHAEL SINCLAIR WALTER DOING A FLYING SIDE
KICK - 1976**

CHAPTER TWO: A LONG ROAD HOME

When they finally pulled me out of the crashed vehicle, paramedics put my right leg in a device that pulled my foot and broken bones back into some sort of normal position. I was taken to South Bay Memorial Hospital via ambulance. Emergency room, here we come.

It was a zoo of confusion, so I was told later. While in the emergency room, one of the doctors working on me, for some odd reason, thought I had no insurance. The nurses and the doctor discussed the possibility of cutting my leg off. One of the doctors said, "Don't waste the time or money. This patient most likely won't make it and he doesn't have any insurance anyway. Let's just send him over to the county hospital to die."

That next day, Dave's roommate Sango called my Mom and Dad who where still living in Vermont at the time. My parents called my older brother, who was a little closer to me, in Dallas, Texas. My brother was the first of the family to see me. I was in a coma for three weeks. During that time, my brother had conflicts with the friends in my life who were visiting me in the hospital. They wanted to help take care of my personal business while I was laid up. They were like my second family, and they were upset with him because they knew of the strain that existed in our relationship over the years. (Recently, both my brother and I have come to peace over my past behavior.)

Then my dad came out. During the first couple of weeks that I was in the coma, I was very restless. I had a 60 pound, full-length cast from my foot to my hip. I was in traction, but I was moving around a lot. At one point, I started hitting the cast with my right hand, and then I held my hand up and raised two fingers. This confused both my family and the doctors. Then all of a sudden, my heart stopped and I flat-lined. Yes, I had died. I can describe this because it was all told to me later, but I hold myself accountable for the story as it goes into much more depth. The surgical nurse had told me a lot, but I have something to tell that no one else knew had happened.

As the doctors and nurses were working to save my life, I had an out of body experience. I left my body when I died. As I floated through the air above the bed, I saw a great light, but it was not white; it was light gray. My body stopped at what appeared to be a wall before passing through to the outside of the building, but is was not a wall, it would be the ceiling. I stood upright on top of the hospital roof and looked out over the Redondo Beach area and the ocean. An angel appeared to me in a gold robe, I was very relaxed, I was at peace not scared at all. The angel took the gold robe and placed it around my shoulders so I would not be cold. I looked up into the light and then back to the angel, who had no face but did have a voice. The angel put her arm around me and turned me around. We both were looking down at the roof when all of a sudden, I saw my family and friends through the roof.

People were crying, and I looked very bad off. I had multiple skull fractures, was legally blind in my left eye, deaf in my right ear, and had broken my jaw, shoulder, and five ribs. I was paralyzed from the waist down and had multiple compound fractures in my right leg and multiple skull fractures. All-in-all, I was one very messed up dude, hooked up to several machines and life support systems. How did I know all this about the accident? It was in the medical report, and the police report.

As I looked down at my body, family and friends, the angel said, "In a female voice "A decision is being made about whether you are to come with me or go back to them."

I said, "I want to go with you; it will be better for me if I do." The angel said, "Michael, it is not about you or what you want. It is about other people, what they need, and what you all will learn from this."

What seemed like minutes on the roof with the angel, was actually two full days. The doctors got my heart started again, but I just laid unresponsive. My brother called the local Catholic Church and asked to have a mass said in my name and to have a priest to come to the hospital and give me the last rights before I died (again). The doctors told my family that I had a million in one chance of surviving and that even if I did come out of the coma, they believed I was brain dead, that I would be a vegetable, and unable to walk. There was a lot of commotion around my bed. Later, my father told me that I raised my right hand and began hitting the cast. Then I raised my hand again and held up one finger, then a second finger. There was excitement and confusion. The doctors said it was a good sign that I was responding.

My father said, "You're wrong. He is asking us a question and we have to figure out what he is asking." My father had to get into my head to figure this out. I am close with my father, and he knew where to find the answer.

The next day he went down to the beach, that has always been my favorite place to be and think. He stayed awhile and then went to a local church, not realizing it was the same church my brother had called to ask for a mass to be said for me. After the sermon, the priest asked the crowd if they would please have a silent moment of meditation for Michael S. Walter of Torrance, California, who was in a horrific car accident almost a month ago. "Mr. Walter is in intensive care," he said, "with a million in one chance of survival."

Right then, my Dad knew what I had been asking as I hit my cast. He rushed back to the hospital, walked into the intensive care unit, and saw everyone around my bed. He said to them all, "I know what Mike is asking." He looked into my brother's eyes and asked, "What has Mike done all his life?" My brother shrugged his shoulders. My father said, "The martial arts. Mike is asking us if he has one leg or two! We have to convince him he has both his legs or I believe he won't wake up. He would rather die than not be able to have use of his body and his legs." My father looked down into my open eyes and said, "Mike, if you can hear me, grab my hand." I did just what he had asked. Everyone was amazed! The doctors and nurses could not believe what they had just witnessed.

My father grasped my hand. "Michael," he said, "squeeze my hand if you understand me." I squeezed his hand. Then my father said, "Son, listen to me, don't do this to us. You are a part of me. You have fought tougher things before in your life than this tree. Why don't you prove to me you have the guts these people say you have and fight this?" I woke up the next day.

One week later, Jackie, the waitress I told you I was seeing, walked in to visit me. She smiled and said, "Well you always wanted to be famous!" I looked at her in an odd way. She continued, "Mike, you're all over the newspapers and TV. They're talking about the police chase and your crash."

I smiled and said in a rough voice, "What are you doing here?" It was still hard to talk. She said, "Michael Walter, I love you, but you're crazy. I got back with my ex, but I want you to know something. You really rocked my world, superman. But I am telling you this, please Michael listen to all these people and you will get well." Then she kissed me, turned, and walked away. I never saw or heard from her again. I'm sensitive when it comes to things like that—I miss old friends; I miss old times. You know, it still gets to me and all this happened so long ago.

I guess that you all are waiting for *strike two*. Trust me, it is coming soon. God, there is so much more to tell. After a month and half in the hospital with lots of cards and letters, even from friends in Chicago, I was told by the doctors that I needed to go back east and recover at my parent's house in Vermont. I was very weak, so weak that even just a sneeze would cause me to pass out. My weight was just around one hundred and nineteen pounds. They told me I would be able to lie down on the plane (a five-hour flight), but that never happened. I had to sit up the whole way back. Fortunately, my Aunt Jeanne, who was a nurse at the time, came with my mother for the flight. The recovery was going to be a long road ahead. I knew it and so did my parents. We got to Vermont and as we drove from the Burlington airport to my parents house in Montpelier, I was surprised at my surroundings. I had almost forgotten what a beautiful place it was this time of year. However, I was a wreck. I couldn't sleep. I made strange noises when I breathed because of the hole in my throat from a tracheotomy. Most of my life, I depended on myself, even as a kid. Now however, my Dad had to bathe me and my mom had to feed me baby food. I couldn't even go to the bathroom by myself, I was a real mess.

It didn't take long in this small town for everybody to know that I was back and what had happened. My time in recovery gave me a lot of time to think and write. It was also the longest time in my adult life that I went without walking on my own—almost a year. I was a basket case. I think I was in the wheelchair for six months. Since that time, my views have changed a great deal. When I see other people in wheelchairs or bedridden or worse... Well, like the song says, you don't know what you got until it's gone. I tried every day to walk, and every day, I failed. I was told one thing, then another. On one side, it was, "You will never be able to walk again." And then on the other side, it was, "Maybe in a year or two, you might be able to stand." Then there was my side. I told everyone I would be running again in a year. I know this perspective was really hard on my parents and all of my family. Through this book, I hope they can now know how sorry I am for what I put them all through. This is a healing tool for me. I hope, for those who read these words, they will find comfort in the fact that we really aren't alone. We all go through this, one way or another. It's called life.

The next eight months would be a hell like I'd never known before. The pain, the dreams, the attempt to take my own life, the depression, my addiction —they all would raise their ugly heads again and again in different forms. Finally, one day, I looked into the mirror and for a moment, I was courageous and told myself that enough was enough. I had to stop feeling sorry for myself and throwing a pity party because no one else was coming. No one held that bottle to my mouth, put that cocaine up my nose, or forced me into that car that night, nobody but me. And nobody but me knew what to do now. I told myself, "Get up off your ass and out of this wheelchair and make something of your life, because God don't make junk and He's not through with me yet. He did not bring me this far for me to quit."

I wanted to ask the doctors if I could start using a walker and if I could join the local gym. It just so happened that I had a doctor's appointment that afternoon where they were going to burn my skin together because there was too much tissue damage to stitch. God it's disgusting, the burning of dead skin. I asked the doctor if I could start using a 4-sectional walker, and he said yes you can try. When I asked if I could join the local gym, he said no. I pleaded, but he refused. He looked at my mom, then back at the disappointment in my face. That was enough. He said okay, but only with supervision, and I was only allowed to do upper body exercises. He even wrote me a note and all.-After the doctor finished "welding" my skin, my mom and I headed home. We were very close to a town called Barre, Vermont. At that time, there was only one gym within two towns it was called Pro's Gym. We pulled up to the gym, and both my mom and I started across the ten-foot journey from the car to the door of the building. I call it a journey because it took a little time to move, to get out of the car into that wheelchair. My mom, as always, was very patient and helped me open the entrance to the building. She wheeled me in, and I shook my head. The gym was on the second floor of the building and there was no elevator, the staircase in this old building look like at leased thirty flights of stairs. My mom said, Michael we could come back another time with help because it was going to be difficult to get up to the gym with just the two of us. I told her,"We can do it." She was nervous but agreed to try. It took what seemed like forever, but we made it. We reached the top of the stairway, and that afternoon, I signed up at Pro's Gym in Barre. I don't think it is still there today. To the normal eye, all that was happening looked good, but I was still having bouts of depression. To me, my recovery was not happening fast enough. I didn't have the guts to fight off all this negativity I was bringing on myself—not yet. I was still dealing with my house, motorcycle and belongings in California. All this and not making any money was getting to me. It was just not happening.

Six months went by and I had been staying in touch with almost everybody in California. I was getting around on the walker finally, and I was managing the stairs by belly crawling up and coming down on my butt. My parents were feeling better about everything. Sometimes they would leave me alone in the house and go out for an hour or so, but I had to promise I would stay on the main level of the house. One day, my mom and dad went out to the store and I was watching old martial arts video tapes. It just so happened that my father was a hunter, and he had many rifles downstairs in the basement. They were always locked up, but I knew where the key was. I was sad, tired, depressed; I wanted to end it all. I didn't think there was any reason to live anymore, so I went downstairs on my butt and made my way across the floor on my belly. I worked myself up to my feet, balanced by the wall, and found the key to the gun rack. I unlocked the rack and removed a rifle. I took a bullet from the gun rack drawer loaded the rifle, and placed it on the floor pointing up to the ceiling. I put my mouth over the top of the barrel of the rifle and began to cry. I started to have flashbacks of my life, my friends, high school, Margie, Joanne, pets, my parents, my brother, my two sisters, my car accident, and that of the angel. As I reached down for the trigger to end it all, out of the corner of my eye, I saw Dad standing there.

I heard him say, "That's right, son. Take the easy way out." I said, "They told me I would never be able to walk again, Dad! I can't take this anymore."

My father then told me what he had said when I was in the coma. He said,   "Michael, don't do this to us. You're a part of me. You have fought tougher things before in life before then this tree. Why don't you prove you have the guts these people say you have and fight this?"

I took it as a challenge and put the gun off to the side. When I looked back to my dad, he was not there and never had been. I didn't want to die and in my last moments, what he said to me when I was in my coma is what pulled me through again. *Yes, this is strike two.*

I had hit my bottom. I wanted out of this hell I created. I put the gun back and got upstairs. When my parents came back home, all was back as it had been. All except for me — something had happen, something had changed I had really changed.

The next day, I started working out the best I could. Before the accident, I could lift 275 pounds in what is called a military press (a lift over my head), and I could bench press 400 lbs. After the accident, when I first began working out again, I could only lift two pounds. I could only ride a tenth of a mile on an exercise bike with a half cast on. Before the accident, I could run six miles. Even pull-ups had been reduced to a single repetition. I think you get the picture. However, I would not quit—not now, not ever. Another six more months passed by. I went from a wheelchair, to a walker, to crutches, to a walking cane, all in a year. Where once there had been doubt, all of these results started to take place. Call it what you want. I call it what it is—a miracle from God.

My weight increased from 119 lbs to150 lbs in that year. I went from almost killing myself to feeling very strong in all ways. When I told my family and doctors I planned to move back to Los Angeles, they all told me that in their views, that was not such a good idea. I told them it was something I had to do, that Danny, Richard and Art were all back at the Kali Academy and they would not always be in my life. I told them I had to go back to face my own personal fear and demons, I had to face my own fears—my own fire, the fire deep with in all of us. I had to face the fire. I hoped they could and would under-stand one day why I had to do this. It was a very sad time.

In a few days, I was headed back to Los Angeles. Mona, a good friend, picked me up from the airport. Crowds made me nervous. I carried pic

KALI - DEMO - PITTSBURGH , PA - 1998

tures of my accident in my wallet, and I was not at all over what had happened to me. As Mona and I drove away from the airport, she asked if I wanted to go back to my house. I said that I wasn't ready yet, so I asked if I could stay at her place for a week or so until I got things sorted out. She agreed. That week, I would look for a job and pick up my motorcycle. Later that same week, I stopped by the Kali Academy to visit with Mr. Danny Inosanto.

A plumber that I knew hired me, but I think he just felt sorry for me. He put me to work doing office stuff and fixing faucets, work that mostly allowed me to stand up so that I didn't have to get under houses or use much strength.

Sifu Dan and I started meeting a couple times a week to talk about life, death, and Bruce Lee. We also talked about what I was going to do for my life's work now that my boxing and MMA career was finished. Others in the school thought I was getting private lessons and I never said anything different. Sifu Danny, that is how we addressed him at the school, taught me so much in that time about very deep stuff. I told him, "I want to start training again."

He asked, "Where?" I said, "Here." He smiled and said, "Michael, I understand, I really do. But you can't train here anymore, Michael. I don't have that kind of insurance to protect you." I said, "Sifu Dan, I will sign a waiver. I don't care I need all this, sir. I need you "

"Michael," he said, "after meeting your parents, I would not feel right about letting you back in the kickboxing class. Michael, you might die if I did, and you know that. But I have an idea."

Surprised, I asked, "What, sir, what?" "Hold on," he said. "How about if you start in the stick and weapons class and see how you do in there? No promises. If you mess up or get hurt one time, you're out. Do you understand me? "Yes sir, Thank you, Sifu". Then he said, "Michael, in a year, if you do well, I will invite you to the Kali demo in Hawaii to meet one of my instructors. It won't be easy, Michael. You have a challenge, an all up hill battle."

"Sifu sorry I don't agree, sir. You see, since my accident, life is all downhill from here on out." Danny smiled - point made.

Time had passed by, almost a year, and it was getting close to Christmas. All my family was back east. I was working as a plumber. I was strong, still on my cane, but getting around well. I was getting ready for the demo in Hawaii. Yes, Danny had invited me. It was a great honor. I would be on the Los Angeles JKD / Kali Demonstration Team.

I started dating a girl that my roommate and co-worker, Tony G, introduced me too. Her name was Candy. She had a brother who was just getting out of jail and another brother who was an actor. Candy's mom died right about the same time as my car accident in 1980, and it was now 1981. She was really messed up about losing her mom. At that time, I had no idea how that must have felt. (I do now) I had lost friends and distant family, but not a close family member. All the time since my car accident, I had not touched a drink or a drug. When Candy and I started dating, we would go for rides on my motorcycle and would talk about what happened to me and how I lived through it. Then I said, "We all have emotional issues". I thought maybe with what happened to me just a very short time ago, it might have been helpful to her in some sort of way. I would be so very wrong.

One night I walked up to her door, she and her brothers had a house in Redondo Beach, close to 190th street. Remember that street? One of brothers had just gotten out of jail and was staying there, but was not home at the time. Her other brother, the actor, was home. I knocked on the door, he answered it, and invited me in. We talked for a few minutes, and I asked if Candy was home. He informed me that she was sleeping in her room. I remember looking across the room and saw her bedroom door was closed. I said good-bye and asked her brother to have Candy call me later. He said he would. I walked right by her room, out the door, got on my motorcycle, and drove away. I thought it odd that my bike didn't wake her up, but I just let it go.

The following day I went to work and when I got home at the end of the work day, I changed my clothes and then headed to the Kali Academy to work out. Just as I was going out the door, the phone rang. I answered it, and on the other end of the phone was my roommate, Tony G. He told me that Candy's brother Chip, the actor, had just come home from work. There was a pause on the phone. I said, "Okay, and ...?" Tony then said to me, "Mike, Chip found Candy dead of an overdose in her bedroom."

"NO! OH GOD NO! Damn it, Tony, NO! She was just sleeping last night. That's what he told me. I was there last night." I dropped the phone—I was in a daze. I don't remember the timeline involved, but I do remember I drove away in the plumbing truck. It was parked outside my house because most of the time when you work for a plumbing company, you take your work truck home. Anyway, I took the truck for a drive. Now remember, I had not had a drink or had a drug since my car accident, but that was all about to change.

Looking back and reflecting on my behavior at that time, I would say that I was very confused about life. I didn't go to Candy's house, I didn't go to the police station, and I didn't go to the morgue. I went to a bar and got drunk and tore the bar apart. I got into a fight with some bikers. All of a sudden it seemed my life and actions were right back where they had been before my car accident. I went crazy. Why the police were never called on me, God only knows. I think one reason is that they knew me at the bar. The second reason is because I called Tony G and he showed up with one of our buddies. I don't remember how, but he took the coil wire off the engine of the truck so I couldn't drive it.

I never went to the funeral and well, that monster I thought I had put to rest inside me, that had caused such troubles over my life and in the lives of my family and friends, had just woken up and was ready to raise as much hell as could be raised.

The next day I didn't go to work, but that afternoon I did go to the Academy to work out. I remember as if it was yesterday. I walked into the Academy, and I had a mean, bad-ass look on my face. Somebody I knew who also worked out at the Academy and knew Candy, heard about what happened and told Richard Bustillo, my instructor. I was punching the heavy bag with no bag gloves on. I was hitting the bag so hard my hands were bleeding and tears were rolling down my cheeks. People in the Academy were just keeping their distance.

Richard saw what was going on, he walked over to me and said,"Michael, I heard what happened to your girl-friend, and I am so deeply sorry, but I really mean what I am about to say. You can stay here and workout and beat on this bag till your hands fall off. But you will work out alone tonight. You will not work out with anyone else. You won't fight anyone; you won't use weapons with anyone, not tonight. Maybe tomorrow, but not tonight, is that understood?" He looked straight into my eyes. "Michael, is that understood?" I answered "Yes sir."

I started to train harder than I ever had in those months to follow. Don't get me wrong. I was doing any drug I could get my hands on. I would have relationships with any female that would have me. Now I was going from one job to another—bouncing, bodyguard work, and working for a private investigator. I was on a self-destructive path to hell. In time, there would be an abrupt stop to this destructive behavior. I wondered how this behavior could start and then continue after all that I had been through. I thought—with my belief in God, what I had put my parents and my family through, would be enough to keep me from ever doing that again. People say that the definition of insanity is "trying the same thing over again, expecting different results". Well, I was a little insane and out of my mind with guilt and shame. However, I will tell you what I learned from this tragedy. That night I went over to see Candy and her brother Chip said she was sleeping, I should have just knocked on her door. I might have been able to save her life. There was a reason why she didn't wake up when my loud motorcycle roared in and pulled up outside of her house that night. I should have listened to my gut feeling. Today I try to do just that.

Christmas Day of that same year I went over to the only place I knew where to find the answers, the Academy. I had a key to the Academy, as did some of the senior students, so I went there to work out. I was on the floor working out with a special brace on my leg when all of a sudden, Danny Inosanto walked in. He looked at me in a very odd way and said, "Michael, what in the world are you doing here? It's Christmas!" I answered, "Sifu, this is all I got. My family is back east, my girlfriend is dead—this is all I got."

Danny walked into his office, sat down behind his desk, and called me into his office. "Michael, please come in here I need to talk to you."

I got off the floor, walked into his office, and sat down on a couch. I looked around his office, it was like a shrine. There were walls filled with personal pictures of Bruce Lee and other famous martial artists. I love this man Danny Inosanto, to this day. He might not know it until he reads this book, how much he helped me in those days just by being my friend and not judgmental. Danny was not just a great teacher but a true friend, both he and Richard. As we continued to talk in his office, Danny told me that he wanted to introduce me to a stunt coordinator friend of his who was also a great martial artist, a guy name Bobby Bass.

After we come back from Hawaii, Danny said to me "Michael, you have done unbelievably well in your recovery from your car accident. You can't be thinking of making a living for yourself in this business. I think you could do well in the entertainment business." Then I asked, "As what?" "As an actor and a stunt man" he said.

Note:

I saw Danny in 2005. He was one of the judges in the Maryland National Open, a martial arts tournament where I took second place in the heavyweight division in full contact stick fighting.

I smiled and thought that seemed cool. So we went to Hawaii and had a great time—great memories. We did a couple of demos and then came back to the mainland. I moved away from the South Bay Area of Southern California and up north to the San Fernando Valley. Then I moved to Van Nuys and into a one bedroom apartment. At that point, I started working in a bar as a bouncer. I also got a job working for a plumbing company, and I would finally meet Mr. Bobby Bass.

I'm jumping to 1982. I know I have left some things out of my story. Some I've forgotten, and some I feel are not that important. However, I hope the things I am telling you are helping you understand why I acted the way I did. This is a big deal to me. I am telling my daughter and the world my story. Now it is up to the world and my daughter to read about it—I did my part.

For the next year, I made many mistakes trying to get doors open in the entertainment industry before I finally started meeting the right people and the right doors started to open. I saw an ad one day in the local newspaper. It was for anybody who wanted to learn to be a stunt man or woman.

WARNING! This is not how anyone goes about becoming a professional actor or a stunt person. When you're trying to make it in the field of entertainment, there are many cons and traps to be careful of, no matter what age or gender you are. The newspaper ad was one such con, and I was as willing or stupid (or both) as the fifty others there who had $600.00 taken from them. The only up side was that I started to learn some pretty cool stuff.

After about two months, the person that took my money told me to go down to the Screen Actors Guild (SAG) office in Hollywood and tell them that I wanted to join. So I did just that. I was headstrong, held my chest out, and when I walked into that office I said, "I am here to join. Where do I pay my union dues?" The lady behind the glass window politely laughed and said, "Sir, you can't just walk in here and join like that." She went on to explain to me that if people were interested in becoming a member, there were proper ways to do it.

So the guy that took my money moved away and if I remember correctly, it had something to do with the FBI looking for him because he had done this scam in other places. Another good thing that did happen out of all this. I met this lady who wanted to become a stunt woman. Her name was Patty B, and we dated for a while. Eventually, we moved in with each other. We both were attempting to make it in the "biz."

I will never forget when I worked on Rocky III. When I went for the interview, the person told me to bring some pictures. I walked into the production office, and a man said hello and asked if the pictures were mine. I said they were. He opened my family photo album, (too funny, thinking back on all this), and very nicely he began asking me what pictures were what. I told him as I pointed, "This one is my mom and dad, and this is my dog, and that one is of the homes back east that I grew up in." He stopped and closed the book and said that they were nice but did I have any black and white 8 x 10's with a résumé. I said, "Excuse me?" "Son" he said, "Are you in the Screen Actors Guild?"

I smiled because I knew that answer, and I said, "No sir, we'll not yet. Is there a problem?"

He said, "No" and wrote down on a piece of paper a phone number for non-union extras. It was a rough learning year, but later on that year I made a call to Mr. Bobby Bass. We would meet at the Palomino Club. What a great guy he was. We talked a lot about the stunt business, the martial arts, and his friendships with Danny Inosanto, Richard Bustillo, and his close friend, Judo Gene LeBell. I was amazed to find out LeBell was also an outstanding stunt man. I had only read about Judo Gene LeBell's martial arts credits and awards.

"Danny told me all about how you were training for and going to try to fight for the middle weight boxing title of the world and about what happened to you in that car accident. Sounds like that would make a great book or movie."

"Well, Mike, I am going to do you a favor because Danny asked me to. He said I would like you and that I would understand you. He was probably more correct than you realize. So tonight, I want you to come down to the movie set I am working on to meet some of the stunt guys and gals. Then later, I want to introduce you to one of the best stunt men in the biz, my buddy, Dar Robinson." He wrote down the directions and the number for his answering service. All the stunt men and women were pretty much on this one answering service. Although there are many phone services today, back then there was only one line to be on, and that was Teddy's. We shook hands and I said, "Thanks" and told him I'd see him later that evening. He looked at me and said, "Don't thank me, thank Danny Inosanto."

I went home, Patty had dinner on. I asked her how her day went. She told me it was okay, and she asked me how mine was. I told her I was very happy. We finished dinner then we both showered and she went with me to the movie set. It was so cool! Some of the stunt guys and girls we met that night were, and still are, some of the most talented people I have ever met in my life. You have to understand, I have raced cars, raced motorcycles, and fought most of my life, but to see how these people did it for the camera was watching true art.

1983

Note:

This is not a "How To" book on how to become a stunt man or woman. There are many tools and tricks in this trade. I will respect my brothers and sisters in this business and their craft by not letting certain things out. I hope you respect and understand my position on this. This book is all about my life and my memories in the entertainment industry.

Patty and I stayed most of the night on the film set, but we both had jobs in the morning and had to leave after a while. Before we left, we were all sitting around in the stunt trailer. Patty and I were listening to all the crazy stories these guys and girls were telling. I was in heaven as the night passed on. When it came time for us to leave, we said our good-byes. I found out later there was a restaurant in Studio City, California that had a sandwich named after Bobby Bass. (Mr.Bass died Nov 7,2001 at the age 65.)

I drove Patty back home. We talked about what had just happened, how we both needed to start buying certain things to help us in the business. We both had to get new pictures—head shots not my family photos (smile). We had to buy a pager because cell phones had not come out yet. A few weeks went by and Mr. Bobby Bass reached me on my pager. There was normally a three year waiting list because you had to know someone to get on Teddy's answering service. I was able to get on sooner because of Mr. Bass. I was working hard as a plumber and a bouncer and enjoying my relationship with Patty. But I was now getting messed up, doing a little too much cocaine and alcohol again—not all the time, but enough to start getting into trouble. Patty was always there and we were both working hard. I was even teaching martial arts classes at a friend's school. I was hustling for stunt work, but I still didn't have my SAG card, so nobody was taking me seriously. The Screen Actors Guild union is hard to get in.

Patty and I decided to buy a house together. We bought a place at one end of the San Fernando Valley in the canyon. It was between Box Canyon and Bell Canyon, an 1800 square foot ranch-style home that overlooked the valley. It was in a gated community with a pool, hot tub, and steam room. We were really sitting on top of the world. One never knows what one has till it is all taken, or thrown away. As I look back on those times I often wonder why, when I had it all, why did I think I needed more?

I remember one weekend the phone rang. Patty was visiting her family in Canada; Patty was not a United States citizen yet. Anyway, the phone was ringing, so I answered it and said hello. The voice on the other end was Bobby Bass. He asked what I was doing today, I said, "Nothing." He asked me if I could meet a friend of his in North Hollywood. He made sure I knew where the location was, which was right down the street from the martial arts school I was teaching at. He said, "Well, how long will it take you to get there?" I said, "About a half hour."

Then he said, "The man you will be meeting is Dar Robinson, the stunt man I told you I wanted you to meet." Bobby quickly changed his mind and explained he had a better idea. I will call Dar and tell him to meet you where you teach. I think it's right around the corner from his house." I said, "Great, tell him that I can be there soon." I hung up the phone and then I called Danny Inosanto and told him everything that had happened since we came back from Hawaii. He was pleased and told me to keep my temper in check and just listen to these two guys. They were two of the best in the business. I hung up the phone and got in my car. Well, it was one of Patty's cars. At the time, Patty made more money and had a better job than I did. I pulled up to the Karate studio in North Hollywood and there, waiting at the door, was this guy I would say was very fit, about 6 feet tall and165 pounds. I parked my car, got out, and walked up to him. He smiled and asked, "Are you Mike?"I said, "Yes sir." He said, "Hello I'm Dar Robinson. Bobby Bass asked me to meet you here."

We shook hands and I invited him into the karate studio. We talked for hours. He then asked if I could do him a favor. I was blown away! "me?" What in the world could this guy need or want from me? Of course I said, "Yes anything. What do you need?" He then told me of a martial arts friend of his that just moved into the area and needed a place to train. He asked if I could work it out so he could train here, being it was so close to Dar's house. I said,"Done deal - no problem."

Then he told me something that rocked my world. Dar said, "You do this for me and I'll see what I can do to get you your SAG card." He said,"A friend of mine is doing a television series called the *A Team*, and I will give him a call, see if I can get you some work on that show. No promises. We will just have to see." (That never happened) Meanwhile, he said, "I know you know how to fight, but I don't think you know how to fight for the camera. It's called motion picture fighting, and its sixty percent of most stunts you will do. The other forty percent is more specialized work like high falls, car work, and then the ultimate stunt—the total body fire engulfment. Getting back to my point on fighting, this is as good as place as any to start to learn."

We both stood up and he began teaching me the art of stunt fighting. Then day after day, month after month, I was learning my new craft. Dar Robinson taught me car work, motorcycles, fights, and fire. Then he saw how well I did on the trampoline, so finally, he began teaching me what he was known the world over for—high falls. I was learning my new-found craft from one of the best stunt men ever in the world at the time.

Please don't get me wrong. Since then, I have met some equally great stunt performers, both men and women. It was just that at the time, all I knew were two. Dar was one of the best ever, and then I met Kenny, Dar's right-hand man. I also met the others on the team. They all would go to a movie set or some live event. I would stay in California and clean Dar's hot tub, or the yard, or look after the house. I was like, hey! What's up with this? So one day when we were working out, Kenny walked by and said hello on his way to the garage where he'd work on some stunt gear.

I turned to Dar and said, "You know, I really want to thank you for all you are doing for me, but I thought you were going to try and get me my Screen Actors Guild card. I never go on the set with you guys. I feel like I'm your little stunt bitch." He laughed "Mike," he said, "you're good. You're really good, but you have a lot to learn about the business. You might think you're low man on the totem pole, and you are. But you are on my stunt team, and I know you don't understand what that means, but there are a thousand guys out there that wish they could be on that totem pole where you are right now."

Then he told me something I tell to everyone that I help learn this business. He said, "Mike, don't rely on me to get you work. I will try to help you get work, but I got Kenny and the guys to look after first—then you. Okay? If you can find another way or a faster way to get your SAG card, more power to you. This is a tough business, Mike. If you need to walk away from me now, I'll understand. Then I will look you up in a couple of years and ask you for a job, because I know you're going to do well in this business. Just remember what I said. It's a tough business and like any business, you have great people and some not so great people."

I hugged him and told him I needed to make it on my own. I thanked him again for all he'd done for me. Then he told me something I will never forget. He said, "Just remember Mike, when you're standing on top of a ten story building looking down, with the cameras rolling, and the director says action—don't assume that just because someone says that there is air in the air bag that there is air in that air bag. Always have a second stunt safety person you know and can trust to be in your corner. Always cover your own ass and check things out yourself."

That was the last time I ever saw Dar alive again. He died in a freak motorcycle accident a few years later. I will never forget what he did for me and how he and Bobby Bass started me off. I have pictures of Dar and Bobby Bass hanging up in my house. I walk by them every day. I did meet Dar's widow and his ex-wife, but never his kids. I heard over the years that one of his sons became a stunt man. At the writing of the first edition of this book, I lived on the East coast and didn't get out to L. A. much anymore. I still had an answering service out there, though not the same one I was with for almost 20 years. I had to change services - everything changes.

When I left Dar's stunt team I heard of another guy who had a team and a stunt school. Back then, old-time stunt men didn't like teaching stunt secrets to anybody outside of family or close friends. It didn't matter if we had the money to pay for the lessons.

There was a conflict in town I didn't know about, so of course I got involved in it. Boy did that upset a lot of people. It seems I had a good habit of doing that over the years. So the relationship with that school didn't last long. Meanwhile, Patty and I made another decision. Because she was not a United States citizen and her work Visa was about to expire (I think that's what she told me), she said, if I married her she would pay me $10,000. And give me one of her cars. She loved me and all, but this was going to be a business deal.

Well, I was drunk when she asked, and I did love her, so I said, "Sure, why not?" I should've stopped drinking then. The whole thing upset my family, they liked Patty, but they just didn't think it was a good idea for me to get married at that time.

I was working a plumbing job and bouncing in a strip club. Patty and I got married so she could become a citizen of the United States. I had a load of money in the bank and a cool car. Time passed, then one night I was working the strip club out by Chatsworth, California and these three men walked in. I don't know or remember why, but I didn't let them in. All of a sudden a big fight ensued, and I put all three of them in the hospital. It was their fault, but it was a not a pretty site.

The company moved me to a steakhouse down the road that they also owned, and I started to work there as a bouncer. Things were going well there. During this time I met a young man named Anthony, who was nineteen I think. We met at this place where some other stunt guys were meeting, and hit it off. As time passed on, we would work out a lot together.

When I lived in Torrance, California I was teaching at a friend's Savate school. Savate originated in Paris, France in the 19th century. Savate is a martial art, a type of kickboxing where kicking as well as punching is allowed. Anyway, sometimes, Anthony and I would work out there together. We became, lifelong friends. Anthony and I worked in several bars all over L. A. We were side by side, getting into many bar fights—some of which ended up out in the streets of Hollywood including one fight on Hollywood Blvd.

Anthony had to bail me out of jail on more than one occasion. So that is how life was for many years. I was married, we were both working, however, I was always in fights. I remember one such night I was in a bar off Roscoe Blvd. in Canoga Park, California. I was very drunk and riding my motorcycle. In this bar, there was a biker yelling at his girlfriend with two or three other bikers standing around the pool table. Well, biker number one pushes his girlfriend, she slaps him, he slaps her—you get the picture. About the time he slapped her, I knocked him out, and then the strangest thing happened to me. The biker's girlfriend grabbed a hand full of hair, bounced my head off the pool table, and down I went to the ground.

I don't care how much boxing, or martial arts training you have, one drunk against three or four not-so-drunk bikers with pool cues—that one drunk loses every time. In this case, I know you know who that drunk was. I don't remember how many boots I took to the head and body that night. I do remember it took over a month for the swelling to go down. (True story.)

I gather after this point in your reading, you're noticing a pattern here with me and my ability, or lack of ability, to be social at a normal level, whatever that level might be. I had removed myself from the state of normality by abusing drugs and alcohol. Patty, God bless her, I think she started noticing a pattern also. She was getting tired of getting up at 3:00 a.m. and bailing me out of jail, when I couldn't get a hold of Anthony—Imagine that!

I just called Anthony, who still lives in LA. I called him to check on some of the details about this story I thought he might remember better than me.

One night I was working the steakhouse, and my boss, Tiger was his name, came running up to me from another part of the restaurant. He said, "Come with me, Mike!" So I ran toward the bar because I thought there was a fight or something. He said, "Not that way, come with me to the kitchen, Mike".   He hid me in the freezer. Remember those three guys I put in the hospital when I got into that fight in the strip club (before I worked at the steak house)? Well, somehow they found out where I worked and were hunting me down with metal bars and guns. So there, I froze my butt off until the police showed up. (True story.) Sometimes even I find it hard to believe, and I lived it!

Well, I thought of a great idea I needed a change. My friend Anthony worked at a bar on Hollywood Boulevard called the Seven Seas, so he got me a job there too. I don't know if it is still there today. When heavy metal ruled in the 1980s, a lot of bands would come into the club to drink and do other recreational activities; it was a wild time.

Anyway I also got a new job with a stunt group that, in time, would turn out to be all right. For the short time I was there, we all worked on a few movies. I got my SAG card working on a movie called Metal Storm with Kelly Preston. Some very famous people came out of that film whose names I can't remember. If you rent it, you'll see who they are and you'll see my name in the credits under stunts. I got my SAG card in June of 1983—then I started working all the time. I was doing extra work right before my car accident. Now, a few years later, a star was born. I am *so* just kidding. Anyway, for me and Anthony, training was very important. We both were new in the business so we would practice all the time—high falls, fighting, those fire burns we had learned, and of course, driving stunts.

It is time to come clean about something I had forgotten to tell you. I told you I got to California around 1974. In 1976, I got my first of four or five Driving While Intoxicated (DWI) charges. So in 1976, I had to go to Alcoholics Anonymous (AA) meetings, and I did not mix in well. I didn't like all that stuff and all the "poor me" crap. I did like the way these people stayed sober—well some but not all. You ever see the movie, Fast 'n Furious? I wasn't in it, but that was how my life went—a quarter mile at a time. I was a runaway train on my way to a wreck. There is one thing above everything else, when you suffer from an addiction of any type. Your body wants to stop and your mind says, NO I don't care what your body wants. You will do what I want, and I want more! And there goes the cycle and a simple definition of a lifelong puzzle. I am attempting to be as honest as I can and also to protect certain people as I tell this story.

Patty and I did get married, but after about a year or so, the marriage was falling apart—imagine that! Patty was now seeing someone else. Please don't feel sorry for me, because I wear no halo on my head. I was seeing Cindy, the waitress I had met at the steak house. What a twisted web we weave when first we practice to deceive. Pretty sick huh? Patty knew I was with someone else, and she knew that I knew she was with someone else. Then we would sleep in the same bed with each other at night. But the love was gone from our relationship. I bet you thought this was *strike three* or it would be coming up soon. Nah! There are more pages before that happens but trust me, it happens. And if you have made it this far and stayed with me, you will not believe how this story ends.

I am getting tired. It is 11:07 p.m. EST. I started writing the first edition of this book on September 11, 2006, writing for long hours every day. It's fun, and I promise you I will not let you down. Hopefully you'll even learn something that might help you in some manner in your life along the way, or you maybe know somebody who could get something out of reading this. I will say good night and look forward to being with you in the morning.

Good morning! It's 7:00 a.m., and I had a great night's sleep. Hope you did as well. This is a great place, this place where I'm writing. I bought an investment property with my sister Donna in a very rural, small town in the state Maryland. The house is 106 years old and all re-done - very cool. I get a lot of peace and quiet here. During the past couple of days, I got a callback on Die Hard 4. What that means is that last week I had a call for an audition on a movie that is filming in Baltimore. They liked the interview, so I got a second one. That's called a "callback." It doesn't mean that I have the job, it just means that the people in the casting department in the production office liked what they saw in me and are considering me for a role in the film.

Back to my story in California...

Well, time passed and I started getting movies and some TV work, stuff like *TJ Hooker*, *Dukes of Hazard*, *Cagney and Lacey*, along with other films. I would go down to the Burbank Studios and Universal Studios mostly looking for work, meeting stunt men and women and stunt coordinators. Then one day everything hit the fan. I drove back down to Torrance, California, where I use to live to visit Danny and Richard and some of my old friends. I had a short visit with Danny and told him all that I had been doing and how he was all a part of it. Then I left to go see Richard, however he was out of town. Then I went to see an old cocaine buddy - huge mistake. I had to work on a movie the following day, *Repo Man*. My buddy Craig, and I started doing lines of cocaine and drinking beers. He didn't have a movie to do the next day. Anyway, a long time passed by, hours it seemed, and we were both very messed up on cocaine. So, as I had no common sense at that point, I started the drive back to the Valley late that night. It was about a 40 mile drive if my memory serves me correctly. I remember being not that far from my house when a police car pulled me over and I got arrested. I did get my one phone call so, I called my wife to come please bail me out of jail. We talked a bit and then she came and picked me up at 2:00 or 3:00 a.m. I had a morning call time for the movie like at 8:00 a.m. Patty and I talked outside in the parking lot of the police station. I wasn't surprised nor could blame her for what was about to come out of her mouth. She informed me that she had enough and wanted to get a divorce.

I, being of sound mind, said,"Sure, and can you drop me off at my car? She told me the police officer said you needed to pick it up in the morning.

I said,"Patty, I have to get my car. I have a morning call time in a couple of hours."

She didn't like it but she didn't have the energy to fight over it. It was my life, so she did what I asked and took me back to my car that was on the shoulder of the freeway. I was still drunk, but as soon as I was sure she was finished talking to me I got in my car and drove back home. I knew if I would go to sleep I would miss my call time, so I did the next best thing. I had beer at home so I stayed up drinking. Yes, I really did—true story. I drove to the movie set that morning, had breakfast, met who I needed to meet, checked out the car I would be in, went to my trailer, locked the door, and went to sleep. Needless to say, I really ticked off that stunt coordinator and I never worked for him again—believe me. Could you blame him? (Sorry Eddie.)

Patty was a real trooper about all of this. I guess it was because she knew she was getting out of it. About month later I went to court, was found guilty of whatever the charges were, and now I had to go back to AA. So picture this: I was working as stunt man, I have a job plumbing, I work in a bar on weekends, and I had to go to AA. Yes, I was a very busy man my poor family, my poor wife - I was always calling and telling my mom and dad what I was doing on the positive side, not about jail and drugs or Patty leaving me. They would find all this out in due time.

Well, Patty did left me, we sold the great house in the Canyon, I moved in with Cindy, and Patty got an apartment in Encino, California. I got the car Patty promised me, and was working a lot in the stunt business. I quit my plumbing job and had to stop working at Seven Seas because of some complaints the management was getting about some crazy bouncer. I don't think I need to tell you who that was. I only wish I knew now what I didn't know then about life, police, drugs, and a code of ethics. Time would pass, I was in the AA program and not drinking for almost 90 days because alcohol has a negative effect on my behavior, or the other way around. I was living with Cindy, whom I found out was a major cocaine dealer in L.A.

Let's backtrack a bit. Do you remember when I was living in Redondo Beach and working for another cocaine dealer and what happened to me because of the effect that the abuse of cocaine and alcohol had on me? It was one night at a beach party about three years past, do you remember? I am glad you do, because I surely had forgotten. I was off to the races again and living with Cindy, I might not have been drinking, but I was sure doing a lot of cocaine and in time I was back drinking again. I have learned over the years that the abuse of either of the above will always result in death, jail, or insanity. If you have been following the story as I know you have been, you're thinking, this has to be *strike three*. No, not even close yet, but it is coming. I had died, I had been in and out of jails, and my behavior was that of a person not acting in a sane manner. Good God! I was so lucky to be alive, to see from my eyes, to hear from my ears, to have the ability to walk, ok maybe with a limp but still, to walk. To be freed from imprisonment, to have the guts to wear my heart on my sleeve and tell my daughter and the whole world my story. And for what you ask? Maybe, just maybe, my story might help or forewarn someone else from making those wrong turns as I have done. Maybe this is why I lived, to share this story. I know it is helping me in ways I never thought of before. If you will, let me speed things up a little.

The year is 1984, the month is July. Cindy was dealing cocaine big time now. I was going on pick-ups and drop offs of money and cocaine, I was what is called a "coke mule." We were living a crazy life, I bought an attack dog a Doberman Pincher, and named him Topaz. This was something right out of the movies. Only problem was, it was all too true - bad guys, police, guns, drugs, money - large amounts of money. During what I like to call my normal hours of the day, I was looking for stunt work, visiting the different stunt groups in town, movie sets, etc., It was the type of job hunting where you would bring your head shot and kiss whatever ass you had to, for a job. One such group was on the second floor of this building. I walked in and there she was, I knew it. Sitting there behind this desk was my next ex-wife (kidding). She might not have known it yet, but I certainly did Chrissy would end up helping me in my career, Become and still is a great friend. We still talk to this day. Actually, I just spoke with her the other night. We laughed when she said, "This book is going to explain a lot to a lot of people."

I said, "YES indeed it's that kind of book." I was not going to point my fingers at any jerks I know in the business. Well, okay, maybe a couple. But I do want to work again. I am only going to tell my story, not theirs, only tell my events—the good, the bad and the ugly ones. At least this book is a true account of those events.

All this time now I also had my bar job, though not at Seven Seas. It was somewhere different because it isn't like I worked stunts every day, and I was not into the system yet to work a TV or movie job and then go on unemployment till the next gig. I did get there, eventually but I was not there yet. So I was working this bar on Ventura Blvd, a very cool and happening place. Everyone went there—movie stars, other actors that wanted to be movie stars, stunt people, and rock-n-roll bands. There were big names like Fleetwood Mac and the likes. During this time I met a man that also had a major impact on my life. Just after I met him, he kicked the living shit out of me, and I have his permission to tell this story. I just called him a few weeks ago and asked. He's a little older now then he was back then, but I have all the confidence in the world that he could kick my ass the same way today as he did in 1983. That's not to downplay my ability on the judo mat or in the boxing ring. I just know what the truth would be. Maybe if I was not trying to kill myself on an installment plan back then on drugs and alcohol, I might have done better in the matches. But it is what it is. He won and I lost "bad." If you are reading this, Judo Gene LeBell, My deep thanks, I learned a great deal from you about life and the movie business, about friendship and about truth. Like I have stated before, I miss old friends and old times, but these are my memories that no one can ever take away. These memories won't fade. They will never ever leave, and for that—I am indebted.

It was on Monday nights that a bunch of people would get together at this college in East L.A. Mr. LeBell would teach a Judo class in the wrestling room at the college. Those were fun times. I remember one week Mr. LeBell asked me if I would go to a Judo demonstration he was putting on that Friday night at Danny Inosanto's Kali Academy. I said I would be honored, it had been some time since my last visit. Well, there we all are on Friday night—Judo Gene LeBell, me, his son David and a few others. The school was packed, I was known very well as you can imagine at the Kali Academy. Anyway, Gene was showing his Judo moves that he had worked out with his son for this demo, then he used his world famous sleeper hold on his son and put him to sleep. I think most of the people there thought it was a set up. But as I know, and as most who experience that hold from Mr. LeBell know, that move is no joke. When he gets his hands on you and puts that hold on you, you're going to sleep. A few minutes went by and then Gene woke up his son. Then it was my turn.

This would be a great learning experience for me. I always thought I could beat Gene. That arrogance would soon become a very painful reality I would come to face. The words he told me that night right before he choked me out have stuck with me to this day. We were out on a wrestling mat with maybe 15-20 onlookers from the Academy, and of course Mr. Inosanto. Gene had me all tied up - my legs, my arms; I couldn't move. He had one of his hand over my mouth so now I couldn't breathe either. Then he grinds his unshaven beard into my chest. I could not tap out to make him stop, but I was being taught a very important lesson.

That Mr. Judo Gene LeBell would tell me the reason why later on, what that lesson was, if I had any trouble figuring it out. You see, he really did understand me, what I was trying to prove as I laid on that mat with the world famous Judo Gene LeBell on top of me. As he had me all tied up he whispered something to me no one else heard, but they saw he was talking to me. It's a funny thing about memories. This story is something I actually think about a lot, even today. He looked me straight in the eyes, his face was maybe an inch from my face, he said, "Michael, you're a talented martial artist and a pretty good stunt man. But you have an ego problem and you still need to learn you can't always win and you won't always win and you won't win tonight against me. You cannot beat me, no one can."

Those were the last words I remember hearing before he put me to sleep – true story. There would be many more life lessons I would learn from that man, and in telling my story. It is also, in a way, to pay tribute to him and my respect to him for all those times he was so willing to teach me, and to be able to say that I fought one of the world's greatest martial artist legends of all time.

It's about the end of the month in July 1984. I had the weekend off from working in the bar. I went to a party. I was still going to AA meetings, and I was not drinking, but I was doing cocaine (that is not how the program works).

I went to a party alone because Cindy was doing something else that night with her friends. When I got to the party, I was very surprised to find out that my ex-wife, Patty was there with her new boyfriend. I was trying to act like a grown-up and not let it bother me. You know, take the upper road. But it did bother me, and then I made a huge mistake. I should've just gone home, but I stayed and was there for hours. Sure enough, I started drinking and got really messed up. Then everybody wanted to go to a bar and finish out the night with dancing. So we all met there at the bar I worked at, and of course, it was a busy night. When I was in the bar, I was handing my business cards out and drinking and doing cocaine in the men's bathroom. So as the night was coming to an end, I was really messed up and got into a pushing match with this guy. He was thrown out of the club. He was outside in the middle of Ventura Blvd. stopping traffic. He was pretty messed up on PCP we found out later. I heard what was going on outside and at the time, I was thinking of my ex, I was so high. Now I was drunk, so common sense went right out the window. I worked my way out the front of the very crowded club. When I got outside, I saw this guy yelling at people and stopping traffic and yelling at the stopped cars. Then he saw me and started yelling and cussing at me. I walked out onto the middle of the street. I walked up to the guy and he threw a wild swing at me. I blocked it. He threw another one. I blocked that one also, and then I threw a punch so hard it knocked him out. He fell so hard when he hit the ground, and he was out cold. I turned around and saw a very large crowd of people that had gathered outside the bar. They all saw what had just happened. I thought for a moment, self defense or mutual combat? Right or am I wrong, which was it? The very next day it would be called first-degree attempted murder. I walked away, left the guy in the middle of the street, blood pouring out of his head, and went home.

I was home the next day with Cindy when the phone rang. Cindy answered the phone and said, "Mike, it's for you; it's the police." I took the call. The police officer told me that the man I had fought the night before was in a coma and he might die, and I needed to come down to the North Hollywood police station. So about an hour later, as I walked into the police station, three police officers arrested me and roughed me up pretty good. Then one officer turned to the other police officers and said, "This is how it should always be done." He was referring to the way the arrest was made. A couple of hours later I was on tier two of the Los Angeles County Jail, charged with first-degree aggravated assault with a deadly weapon (my hands). I called Cindy and she had to call my parents. She told them that she needed help to bail me out of jail. The bail was twenty-thousand dollars.

I talked to my mom from the jail. Now you must understand something. After fourteen years of this type of behavior, I knew my family was getting tired of the phone calls from hospitals, police stations and tired of the emotional, of the financial, of the all around burden I was bringing onto them. But thank God for my parents. They hired a famous lawyer and spent a lot of money. A trial would be held. I was put in an AA recovery house, that was called (Studio 12). I was clean and sober for real for the first time in my adult life. I went to trial, and once again, the God of my understanding showed another miracle in my life. As I stood there in front of the judge, looking at twenty-five years in Chino State Prison, all of a sudden there was a great deal of confusion in the courtroom. The man I had hit and put into a coma that night of the bar fight, had woken up and left the hospital because he had no insurance or cash to pay the hospital bill. He was scared and took off, the police searched for him, but he could not be found, so the charges had to be dropped.

I kneeled down to pray right there in the courtroom. On his way out of the courtroom, my lawyer said to me, "Michael, you have very special parents, and you are one of the luckiest men in the world." I was put on three years' probation, and of course, I had to stay clean and sober.

I had to figure out what I was going to do about my relationship with Cindy and her cocaine dealings. As it turned out, she really wanted to stop dealing and using herself. So she cut her ties in the drug world, and we moved out of where we were living and rented a small house in the San Fernando Valley (on the West Valley). Time went on and both Cindy and I became very involved in AA, (Alcoholics Anonymous) NA, (Narcotics Anonymous) and CA (Cocaine Anonymous) meetings, going to hospitals and prisons to speak and carry the message of recovery. There was even talk about me recording a recovery tape and becoming a circuit speaker. I stopped working in bars and was concentrating on acting, stunt work and my sobriety. At one point, I even worked at a drug rehab hospital. Life was looking bright. I had gotten to work on a TV series called O'Hara. Then there was more TV and more movies like: th *Eye of the Tiger, Jessie, Demon Wind, V,* and *Star Man.* I started to co-ordinate stunts on some films. I loved that the first film I was stunt coordinator on was a film called *King of the City.* After that I worked as coordinator on *Twisted Nightmare.* I started doing action acting roles on shows like *Dangerous Cures* and *Kung Fu, The Next Generation* TV series, on an episode with the late Brandon Lee (Bruce Lee's son). I also worked on a film that

later became sort of a doorman's cult movie called *Roadhouse*, with the late Patrick Swayze.

Four years would come and go. I had four years clean and sober. I was working all the time on TV and film. Cindy and I broke up. I moved and bought a house in Canyon Country and life was good. Dar had died, and that had a pretty big effect on

Me I didn't like earthquakes, mud slides or canyon fires. But my dreams were coming true. I remember one day I was looking for work and I went down to the set of the Fall Guy TV series. I talked to the stunt coordinator and he introduced me to this famous actor, Doug Mc-Clure. We became good friends, and he wanted to hire me as a bodyguard. That never happened. He died of lung cancer on February 5, 1995. I had the honor to work on a series in Florida with him before he died.

Note:

Cindy decided to get clean and sober. Years later she started dealing and using again and was arrested and convicted. Today she's totally clean and sober. I think she has like 20 years clean.

CHAPTER THREE: STARTING OVER

About this time I had two pick-up trucks. I sold as much of my stuff as I could, and the remainder of it I either took with me or gave away. Then I said my good-byes. I towed one of my trucks behind the other and started across the USA again. I had moved thirty-three times in twelve years, and that was in California alone. Now I was starting all over.

I stopped in Dallas, saw some old friends, went to an AA meeting, and saw an old girlfriend's sister. She had a spare room and let me crash for the night. It took three days to finish the drive to Florida – a very beautiful place. The reason I picked Orlando was because Universal Studios was building a new theme park and film studio and, of course, Disney already had one there. I got a really cool townhouse in a place called Marbella Woods, a gated community. It was a really nice place with a pool, clubhouse, and workout room. Across the street, construction was underway for the new studio, but I needed to find some income until I got to know some other stunt people and the studios were finished. Of course, there was Disney and I was on top of all that. There weren't many stunt people in Orlando in 1988. Miami was a different story and I wondered if maybe I should've moved there. But then, my story would not be what it is, and it wouldn't end like it does.

I fell back on the one thing that always pulled me out of a slump. I had all my tools, so I got a job plumbing. As I am sure most of you know, it is very hot in Florida, and working outside is uncomfortable sometimes. Cell phones had not evolved yet - well they had but not to the level of sophistication we know today. There were no computers, no internet, and no world wide web. It was a different time.

I was clean and sober and going to AA meetings. I was having a great time in life. I would go to bars and just have water or sodas. At a local place called The Dart Bar, I met a lady whose marriage had broken up and she seemed very rich. She drove a Benz, had diamonds all over, blonde hair, great body, and as I would find out later, she also had formerly dated a famous professional body builder. Darlene and I had a great time for about a year. It was an on again, off again relationship.

I couldn't keep up enough work to hold on to the townhouse. I could have bought it for $69,000. A year later, after the studio was built, it was going for $110,000. Boy, I wonder what it is worth today! Instead, I got a one bedroom apartment at a place called Kirkman Apartments, just a block or so away from the studios. I worked out at Bally's Health Club, went back to doing doorman work, plumbing, and kept looking for stunt work. I got an agent in Winter Park, Florida. I was going on interviews as an actor and looking for stunt work on my own.

One day I was working out at the gym, which was also close to my apartment. There was a pro female body-builder doing a book signing, and there was a long line of people for the signing. I walked over to check it out and noticed two young ladies about 22 or 23 years of age. I tried to pick one of them up but no luck. Then I figured, what the hell, her friend was cute, too, so I tried to pick her up. We flirted and she gave me her phone number. Her name was Terri, and she was going to turn pro in bodybuilding. She had dirty blonde hair and a great body. She was 5'4," 125 lbs. I left and she followed. We talked outside in the parking lot for what seemed a long time. We said our good-byes and I drove off. Terri called me the next day, and I met her where she worked, AT&T. We hit it off right away started kissing, we clicked. It seemed too good to be true – and I would find out later that it was. Terri went back to work and we told each other we would meet at the gym later. By now I was burned out on relationships and didn't want to get involved, especially since I'd just broken up months prior with Darlene. Terri really was a nice girl. We would meet at the gym after her work day and work out for two or three hours. This went on for weeks, and then one day she dropped a big bomb shell and let me know she was married, do you see a pattern here in my life? But she was not happy and was having troubles. She wanted to know if I would be okay with becoming friends. I should have walked away, but I as usual once again, I was making the wrong choices. So Terri and I became friends. We worked out together, I would see her for lunch, and then the work out times started to become more frequent. After we worked out, she would go home. This went on for some time. Then one day she told her husband she was going to work out at the gym with her girlfriend. Instead, she showed up at my apartment, and we talked inside for a while. We walked outside to the pool and I was laying on one of those long beach lounge chairs with Terri lying between my legs. She asked if I could ever fall in love with someone like her. I said, "Yes, why do you ask?" Well, before she answered I started feeling really weird, you know that feeling you have when someone is looking at you and you sense it. I am real good at that stuff, so I looked over my shoulder and this man was just looking at us, just standing there looking. I had my leg crossed over her leg and I removed it.

Then I said to Terri, "Do you know that guy over there looking at us?"

She turned and looked and then she said, "Oh my God!" I said, "What?"

Then she told me that was her husband. He had followed her. All of a sudden this was becoming a very uncomfortable situation. She said she had to go. I said she should call me if she needed me. She got up and walked over to her husband and they both left. Later that evening there was a knock on my door. I answered the door, and to my surprise, Terri was at the door with some clothes and a suitcase. She said she'd just left her husband, and then she asked me if she could move in for a few days. I said sure, so she came in and we talked until it got late, then we crashed. Again, those were some great days now that I'm looking back and writing about it. I can't and won't blame anyone for the choices I have made in life. In life, a person has to be responsible for actions taken—drunk or sober. You may be asking yourself if I'm sorry for the things and the mistakes I have made in life. My answer is no, but I *am* sorry for the times I repeated the same mistakes. And I'm sorry for the residual effects that my behavior caused to other people and for not learning from them the first time. But all in all, my experiences have made me the man I have become.

Well, Terri and I soon figured out that the apartment we were living in was too small for the both of us, so we moved into a two bedroom unit in the same complex. Terri quit her job at AT&T. I trained her in stunts and helped her get into the Screen Actors Guild, and we both started working. We decided to start a Florida based stunt group. We opened an office and called it.

"THE STUNT COMPANY"

In the next three years we trained new stunt players, both male and female. We gave stunt demonstrations, did corporate events, safety films, television public service announcements, worked and coordinated stunts for major motion pictures—life was great. We opened an office and a training facility. We had martial arts classes three days a week, held safety training seminars for the fire department, paramedics, and police to help them understand about stunts and safety and how stunt safety differs from what they were normally used to seeing in their everyday activities. Terri asked me to marry her. I accepted and we wed. We went on our honeymoon to Sanibel Island, off the coast of Florida. It was a beautiful time in my life. I loved my new wife, I was enjoying my success in the entertainment industry, and it all seemed like nothing could go wrong or that anything could possibly happen that could be any better than how I was living my life. I was now clean and sober over six years and I thought I had a solid, loving marriage started. Terri and I bought a small house, got a dog, and we would soon be starting a family. It seemed like all my dreams were finally coming true in life. But these dreams would soon come to a violent, screaming halt.

About a year and a half passed by, Terri and I started having troubles. I know it always takes two to end a relationship, but believe me I have been blaming myself for years, probably more than I need to. As time passed, I got Terri a job on a film in North Carolina. I knew this stunt coordinator who I thought was a friend. I was wrong. Terri went on the job and was gone for about a month. She had been gone for two weeks. Not communicating with me, I didn't know where she was. This along with other problems would cause us to have words about a divorce. I was worried. Then her older sister called me she was trying to be the middle person, trying to "work things out." She told me how much Terri loved me and that the issues we were having could be attributed to the age difference—I was 12 years older. I will never forget the night Terri finally came home. The house that we lived in had a front door, a side door, and a back door that led to a small fenced-in back yard where we kept our Chow dog named Stunts. She walked in the side door of the house and had a glow on her face. She set her luggage down. I met her half-way in the middle of the living room and we kissed, we hugged, and we kissed again. I was so much in love with her. I could never understand how or why or what was tearing us apart.

The next day Terri fixed breakfast and said, "Honey, do you think I look fat?" And I said, "No you look great!" and she did. Terri had always been a beautiful, fit woman. She was twenty-three years old and very hot looking. Then she asked a couple of days later, "Honey, you sure I don't look fat?" She said, "I feel like I've gained some weight."

I repeated what I said days before, "No baby, you look great."

For a few weeks everything was going okay. We told each other we would try to work things out. Then a day or two went by and she did one of those home tests and told me that she was pregnant, that we were going to have a baby. I was shocked, scared, and excited. We started to go too counseling to try to get help, to work our relation-ship problems out. When the counselor explained to us that it was something with Terri that was causing the prob-lems we had been discussing, Terri lost her temper and stormed out. She would always say it was me, that it was always my entire fault. Today I have come to learn and understand something Bruce Lee used to always say:

We both tried to work things out. I knew she tried the best she knew how I did my best also, but my best was not good enough to hold the marriage together or to hold her in my life. We got into a big fight one night after I had been working a long thirteen-hour day at the stunt office. My back hurt, my leg hurt; I was tired. I came home Terri had fixed a nice dinner, but I was late so we got into an argument because the food got cold. She got very upset; she'd had a rough day too, I guess. Terri was a strong-willed country girl with the guts to say what was on her mind. I loved that about her. However when something is not going to fit, there is nothing in the world that anyone can do to make it fit. Terri walked out on me that night and filed for a divorce that week. We had dated for a year and half and were married for nine months. The divorce would end up very nasty. That night we fought and Terri called the police. I had to leave the house. Stunts, my dog, was in the backyard. I thought that if I had to go, it was because Terri would stay in the house and she didn't want me there—like a peace order.

Well, I slept at the stunt office. It was a big place—fifteen hundred square feet, bathroom, roll back fifteen-foot garage door, three different offices, and a warehouse area. I slept on the concrete floor for a few days. Then the man living next door to our house called me and said my dog had not eaten in days. Terri had left that night and al-though she came back to get some clothes and things, she didn't give a damn about whether or not Stunts was being fed. I called the Marshal's office, asked if someone would please meet me at my house so I could get my dog and some belongings in the house. The house had not been lived in since the night of the fight. Terri later told me she moved up to her mom's house in north Florida.

Terri was pregnant, and we just couldn't work things out. It was a sad time, no doubt, I think about this every day for years. A baby girl was born, Terri named her Kyleigh Lauren on the birth certificate, Terri put the name of the father as "unknown." That hurt, as did the fact that I was not there to see my baby born. I was not there to see the miracle of birth. I was not there to hold the most beau-tiful little girl in the whole wide world.

I had to close the stunt offices down, sell or give away a lot of stuff. Months later, I found this mini-ranch in Mount Dora, Florida for rent with an option to buy. I moved into a trailer on 7.5 acres, with restrictions that you had to build a home within a certain period of time. I started running my business from there. I had 30 members on my stunt team, a very talented group of men and women that included Jim, Gator, Brian, Jill, Lex, Karen, Chris, Tommy, and John, just to name a few. We could do it all—high falls, car work, fire work, motion picture fights, motorcycle work. I believe a few of them are still working in the entertainment business today. I was proud, and I am still proud of each and every one of them, proud to have been part of their lives. I was hard on all the members, both male and female, because it was my responsibility to train, to teach each of them the correct way a basic stunt was to be performed so they wouldn't be hurt or die in years to come. I knew that back then, they didn't understand why I was so tough. I know they all do now. I have sometimes heard stories, or seen some films, with credits of some of the members who had been on my stunt team —movies they worked on or coordinated. It makes me very proud. Safety was the number one priority. It was then and still is today. It was how I learned from Dar Robinson and others, it is how I work today. I used to have a saying, a company saying, "Always remember—safety first for your life or the lives of others may be at stake. Hire professional stunt players, not just a dare devil."

During this time, I got a phone call from an old producer friend in L.A. who asked if I would stunt coordinate a TV series for him in Spain. I said I would love to. Unfortunately, as it happens a lot in this business, the executive producer said he wanted his friend for that position and that I could be hired as assistant stunt coordinator, as well as the lead actor's stunt double (it is a very tough business). I said sure, no problem. I can work with anyone. I've since found out that is not at all true. Before I flew to Spain, Terri (we had not divorced yet) and I were talking a little. She was back and forth from her sister's house in Miami and her mom's house in northern Florida. She was already seeing some guy (I didn't know that at the time). Terri and I met in Orlando for lunch with some of my stunt guys. I was able to see my baby daughter, Kyleigh, for the first time. Wow! I was amazed. I even tried to talk Terri into maybe working things out and getting back together for Kyleigh's sake. She said, "No Mike, you scare me."

She didn't tell me she was seeing somebody already, much less living with him. I would not find that out until years later. Terri and I parted ways after that lunch. We both still cared for each other, but there was just too much pain, too many bad memories to be able to try and fix the relationship—too much water under the bridge. I think the saying goes,"When it's over, it's over." That is a life lesson I learned the hard way.

In the weeks to follow, I boarded an airplane, flew to England and then Spain on a contract for a new TV series called *Dark Justice*. It was 1990. Yes, still clean and sober, I was working out hard. I had been fighting back then in full contact kick-boxing, as well as doing ground fighting, which today is known as MMA ultimate fighting. I was walking a lot because I couldn't really run any more like I did before my car crash. I would swim when I got the chance.

The TV series took place in Barcelona, Spain. It's a very beautiful city with much history, and I celebrated my thirty-eighth birthday there with about five or six of the crew. We lived in a million dollar condo in the city. It was beautiful and had art work on the walls worth in the tens of thousands of dollars. The city was preparing for the

Olympics, which they would soon host. As I told you before, I thought I could work with anyone. The stunt coordinator on the show was also staying in the condo, and we did not get along. I was clean and sober and, well, let's just say he wasn't. We just rubbed each other the wrong way. But he was my boss on this shoot, and I did have to show some respect since he got the job over me. But over the next few months, tensions between us grew. I had to set up certain things that would ordinarily be the lead coordinator's job to oversee. Instead, he sometimes made decisions that could affect my life and the safety of the series while he was high. I am not listing names of people on those projects for a couple of reasons: (1) I want to work again, and (2) to protect others involved.

Three months went by. I had been talking with Terri. I was having trouble with my boss on this shoot, and I was missing home, and there was a war that was about to start a few hours away. By now, you have seen a certain pattern that I have. One day I just said the hell with all of it. Actually, the exact words were much worse. I started to drink after more than six years clean and sober. I lost control one more time in my life and the bottle became more important than my family, my home, my business, my daughter, and my life. Later that week I was to drive a motorcycle under a moving tractor trailer. I would be driving at forty-five miles per hour.

Insane, you might think. Well, this time, I would have to strongly agree with you. It would be the biggest stunt of the series and the most dangerous.

Later that week, in the early hours of the morning (like 3:00 a.m.) this would all come into play. As I sat on a Norton 750 Commando motorcycle at the top of a big hill, I looked about a quarter of a mile down the road toward all these lights and the movie equipment. The production assistant stood next to me with a walkie-talkie. I heard the voice on the other end of the walkie-talkie say, "Action!" but I just froze. Then I heard that word again, but my body just wouldn't move. Then the production assistant holding the walkie-talkie standing next to me said in a low voice, "I don't think the stunt guy is ready to go yet." I turned to him and smiled, and for the next few minutes I just sat there, thinking of my life, my daughter whom I might never see again, my two failed marriages, my ranch, my mom, my dad, my sisters, my brother, my car accident, and my recovery.

A lot passed through my mind in a very short time. Then I thought of a movie I saw once, a movie about a stunt man. It was called *Hooper*, and I knew most of the stuntmen that worked on that movie. I remember this one scene where two actors were playing stunt men in the film. They were going to jump a jet car over a small river or large creek as the bridge connecting the two sides was going to be blown up. There were all kinds of stunt driving and explosions going on, then the car that the two actors were in came to a complete stop. The passenger, who I would come to know, work with, and respect, Burt Reynolds, turns to the driver, Jan-Michael Vincent, and says, "What are you doing?" The driver answers, "This is crazy ... my life is worth more than this." (Of course the jump would not be done with the actors' stunt doubles would be doing the stunt,) The passenger, who was aging and starting to feel old in the stunt business, turned to the driver and said, "No you're wrong. Your life is worth the amount of money that is on the contract you signed to do this job. Right or wrong, good or bad, that's what your life is worth today." Then the driver says to the passenger, "You're crazy!" And then with a rebel yell, he put his foot to the floor of the gas pedal, hit the jet button, and they jumped across the gorge. Then my mind cleared and I turned to the production assistant and said, "Tell them to roll cameras."

He says over the walkie-talkie, "Roll cameras—he's going for it." I heard, "Action!" and I twisted the throttle on that motorcycle and roared down the beautiful streets of Barcelona, Spain. I was traveling at forty-five miles an hour. I would be crossing an intersection where a car would cut me off right as a tractor trailer was driving through the same intersection. The tractor trailer would slam on its air brakes, and that was the window of time and speed of the motorcycle I had calculated would be the safest time to slide the motorcycle under the tractor-trailer and through to the other side. As I began to slide the motorcycle under the tractor trailer, the wig I was wearing to make me look more like the actor I was doubling, brushed up against the bottom of the trailer. I was told later by the director that as I laid down the motorcycle, an unbelievable amount of sparks flashed from the bike as I slid further down the road. They captured that shot on three different cameras. I quit that night because of differences I had with the stunt coordinator and walked away from a $250,000 contract.

I know what you're thinking; I was thinking it too. But if there is anything about me, it's my word. It's about principles and my word and believing in myself. I was not willing to compromise either. It was a lot of money, still is. Oh well next. The war did start as I was headed back to the US From that point on this world has changed. It is different now. However I will stay with the timeline, with the flow, and discuss world events toward the end of this book. So the producers on the show tried to get me to stay but I said no. And that's why now I know I can't work with just anybody. I am human, and not everybody gets along in the world. The stunt community is a wonderful family, but it is a family of many individuals from different walks of life. Both men and women in the field of stunt work are some of the most talented and bravest people you will ever meet. It takes a special person to want to make a living by putting their life on the line, day in and day out, for the entertainment and enjoyment of others.

Although, not everybody can work with everybody, I have since learned. Most of the time it is just good physical fun. Nine times out of ten you get up and walk away, sore, but you still walk away. Then there might come that one time you don't walk away. You get hurt, you lose an arm or a leg, maybe lose an eye. You might get burned or you might even die. We all eventually know that once we get into this business. Many a stunt player better then I has crossed over. I have been fortunate to have been blessed to know, to work with, and to learn from some of the greatest in the business. Like I stated before in this book, these are my memories I am sharing with you. And memories don't leave or fade, and nobody can ever take mine away.

I came back to Florida, then Terri and I got divorced. I would not be able to see my daughter. Terri convinced the court I had a temper and it would be better for all concerned that we just stayed away from each other. The judge granted all that, and then told both of us to stay at all times one hundred feet away from each other. This was one of the saddest and loneliest times in my life. I think you have already figured something out, *Yes Strike Three.*

As I told you before, Terri met somebody and was now living with him. When the divorce was finalized, she married him and soon afterward he adopted my daughter.

I packed up all my stunt gear, sold some of it, gave some of it away. I was out drinking and drugging again. Two of the stunt guys from the group moved with me to Atlanta, Georgia. I felt like a proud parent of thirty qualified people. However, I decided to close The Stunt Company, the group split up and I wished them all good luck.

Along with me, Gator and Diamond Dave (everybody had nick names), moved first to Marietta, Georgia just outside of Atlanta. We all had to get real jobs. Gator got work, Diamond Dave got work, and I fell back on something I knew all too well—working security at a strip club. I also worked at a very famous country bar called Miss Kitty's, where a lot of big country bands played. I believe it was 1991. I couldn't get any movie work yet. I was not making any money. I was fighting, drinking, and I wasn't happy. We all moved around Atlanta a couple of times. Then we got this two bedroom townhouse in south Atlanta. This would become a fun time in all of our lives. God, I miss those two guys. I had one bedroom on the second floor, and Diamond Dave had one, too. Gator slept in the closet under the steps. He said it was all he needed. Those were some funny times. I remember one time I had a date over, and I didn't know Gator was home. The hall bathroom was across from the closet where Gator slept. My date went to the bathroom, and when she opened the door to come out of the bathroom. Gator opened his closet door at exactly the same time. My date screamed. It was too funny. Then we both had to explain to her why he slept under the stairs in a closet. During this time I was drinking and drugging on cocaine. Gator and Diamond were straight, drinking some occasional beers, but I was the loose cannon of the trio. Neither one of them were into drugs, but we were all great friends, no judgment. I don't see Diamond anymore. Gator and I have a lot of history together, a lot (sadly, Gator died a few years ago).

During this time one of my sisters was back in Dallas visiting some high school friends. One of my sister's friends, Margo, had a younger sister I use to like when I was little kid of about 8 or 9. She was asking about me and my sister got Margo's sister's phone number. Low and behold, after twenty-some-odd years we started a long distance relationship, her name was Diane. We started talking everyday on the phone and soon she came to visit me. Then she asked me to come live with her back in Texas—that was a short-lived romance. Then I moved back to Atlanta, I had bought a stunt trailer to haul all my stunt gear when I lived in Florida, and I had a van also. One day I told Gator and Diamond if they wanted to find me I was going back home to Maryland. I tried to make it in all areas of my life, and I was not a better person for it. I had much wisdom, although not using it. However, my wisdom was locked away, drugs and alcohol had imprisoned my mind. I needed structure back in my life. I needed my family, my brother my sisters, my mom and dad, I was, as the song says, going crazy.

A really good friend of mine once said to me, "Mike, you can try but you can never tame a wild animal, and you're wild my brother. No shame in that, you just have to understand that about yourself."

I wanted to stop this roller coaster I was on in life, and there was only one person to do that. It was the same person that bought the ticket in the first place, and that person was me.

It would take another fourteen years of drinking, drugging, and a lot of pain before I would finally win the toughest fight of my life with the drugs.

It has been many years since I have had any drugs in my system (12 years to be exact). Do I still drink today? Hell no, it is not a controlling battle anymore. It is what it is. Call it what you want, I let God be the judge, not people. Not anymore!

CHAPTER FOUR: A ROUGH ROAD

One day I just woke up, and my whole body hurt. My back, my legs—that car crash beat me up pretty bad. I can walk, I cannot run; I work out every day. But I put myself through what some might call torture for twelve years in the boxing ring and on the judo mat. To this day, fifty-five years in the martial arts, street fights, car wrecks, stunt work, jail, two failed marriages, and simply, time— they all took a toll on my body. I hurt, but slowly I am getting better, one day at a time. I had a very active but destructive life, some people say I was dealt a bad hand in life. That is just not true I was dealt a great hand in life. It's what I did with that hand that screwed my life up. I was given breaks yet, time after time I would always do something to mess it all up. We have one shot at this game called life and it's a very short time. Whatever you understand that to be or whatever your beliefs are, you need to believe this. When it's over, it is really over—no joke. I will come back to this subject towards the end of the story.

I moved back to Maryland and stayed with my parents for a while until I got on my feet. I started working again as a plumber, started working on films again; life was picking up. The year was 1992. I got a phone call from that stunt coordinator I met years ago in LA on *The Fall Guy* TV series. He was doing a big picture in Pittsburg and had heard I looked a lot like two of the actors. He wanted to know if I was available for a couple of days of stunt work. Those two days would end up being six weeks. The movie was called *Striking Distance*, staring Bruce Willis. I had a blast, made some great friends, made lots of money, got a little stupid a couple of times, but I always made everybody laugh. There was a lot of stunt work with a very talented stunt team. One night the stunt coordinator told me that the high fall scene from a bridge that I was to do, would have to be put on hold because of the stormy weather they had been having in that area. The Army Corp of Engineers did not think a high fall would be safe because of all the trash and debris in the rivers.

"Don't worry, Mike" they told me, "there's plenty of stunt work for you to do. It's just your high fall has to wait till the river's calmed down and we can get some divers in the water for added safety."

So weeks went by and we worked some days and some nights. I met this girl named Marcie who came to visit the set. She lived in Pittsburgh and was a nice lady. She came down and visited me almost every night that I was working. We started hanging out on my days off. She showed me the town of Pittsburgh. I had visited there before when I was a child. At that time the town was a very dirty city because of all the steel mills. Now all the mills had closed down and the city fathers, and people of the city had cleaned it up. It really is a great city. I almost moved there after the film was over.

Anyway, the way the script reads, I double Robert Pastorelli, who got into a fight with the lead actor, Bruce Willis. If you saw the film you know who I'm talking about, and if you didn't, go rent it. I still get residuals from it.

So weeks have passed by, and the river water had gone down, so I will be doing my high fall off an eighty foot train bridge. One night Marcie came down to see me and to wish me luck. We both went into my trailer and she wished me luck. Luck would last about twenty minutes— the trailer was rocking. When we came out, the Teamsters were laughing and applauding. (True Story)

After the high fall stunt was performed, people would later tell us that when my and Bruce Willis stunt doubles bodies hit the water, it sounded like a .410 shotgun going off or a small explosion. The rescue boat and divers found the first stunt man who fell off the bridge, but it was not me. I had the wind knocked out of me and was down in fourteen feet of water. It seemed my body had paralyzed and I could not move at first. I just lay motionless in the water. I did manage to surface and then the stunt coordinator and the stunt safeties pulled me out of the water and onto the rescue boat. You should really hear what it sounds like when a 200+ pound man falls from that height into water and then isn't able to breathe; it's an odd sound. So that was it for me—I was done working. Actually, I was done working for about two and half months to be exact. I had broken some ribs and tore my hamstring muscle in one of my legs when I hit the water with such an impact.

There's more. I came back home to Maryland and was seeing doctors for those two and half months. The day the doctor released me, the production office called from L.A. about the movie I was working on. They asked if I was able to work yet and if I could come out to L.A. to finish that scene. I said I would. I went home and packed a suitcase, and off to L.A. I went. Arriving in California, I went to work at the Sony Picture Studio Lot. There, I had to stay in a tank of water for 13 hours, I was pretty much in the water all day with Bruce Willis, where we filmed the final scene of the fight where my guy dies. So picture this: I have a forty-pound weight belt on and a small air bottle called a pony bottle in my jacket pocket in case something goes wrong. In this final scene I had to act like I was drowning in the eighteen-foot water tank, and it had to match the look of the river in Pittsburgh where I fell off that bridge months earlier. So here is how it played out. I am fighting Bruce Willis and he puts a stun gun into my mouth and shocks me (not a real one) and I drown; then the movie ends. We did it on the first take. Everybody loved it, but the director wanted to see it again. It was take two. Then it was one more take for safety, take three. Okay, let's get a close up, take four. Man, this director got a lot of footage on that scene, and I am getting worn out.

The stunt coordinator asks me."You got one more left in you?" I nod my head yes. He agreed, and tells that to the director. This is the last one. The director says,"You ready Mike?"

Note

Selling out is a word in the stunt business when you perform and make the stunt as real as you possibly can.

Point to be made—I was drowning. I had accidentally swallowed a mouthful of water. I reached for my pony bottle, stuck it in my mouth, purged it to clear any air, and started to breathe, but I made a small error. When I started to breathe in the air, I sucked in more water, and now I was really drowning. The stunt coordinator heard and saw all this on a TV monitor and yelled to one of his sons, also working as a stunt safety. They were already in the water and dove down to grab me, and saved my life. Thanks guys—I owe you one.

Well, that's a wrap. I said my good-byes and said, "I'll see you on the next one." I meant I'd see them on the next movie. Off to sleep I went so I could catch a plane back east in the morning, I love this business.

In 1992 I had a great year, both personally and in stunt work. I had a battle going on in my head. I thought about my daughter every day. Terri was re-married now, and I let Terri talk me into letting her new husband adopt Kyleigh. She told me it would be the best thing for my daughter. I talked to my mom about it and she said, "Mike, Terri is the natural mother and I am sorry to say this to you, but Terri is right this time."

I had no clue where in this country they were, and I agreed. I would see Kyleigh three times in my life. The first time would be when Kyleigh was two months old and then when she was two years old and I was living in Atlanta. Then in Maryland when she was thirteen years old.

After that, I worked a commercial in Baltimore, Maryland, where I had to do a lot of stunt driving and jump a pick-up truck a few times. I also set up a lot of the camera shots. This helped me have the chance to get into the Directors Guild of America for my work on that commercial and some other 2nd unit work on films I had done.

It was 1994 and life was good. I was acting, doing stunt work, directing commercials and public service announcements. I had moved into an apartment complex in Annapolis that was just like the TV show, *Melrose Place*. Gator came up from Atlanta and moved in with me. Summers in Annapolis are the kind you don't forget; I love that town. As I am sure you know, Annapolis is the state capitol of Maryland and is home of the United States Naval Academy. Downtown Annapolis is very historic and a very happening place all year around, but the summer time is just great fun. There is an international boat show, international boat races, and if your downtown in Annapolis there are all sorts of shops, restaurants, and bars. I was in one of my clean and sober bouts where I would still hang out with friends and go clubbing, but I was in NA and AA.

I met a lady, and we hit it off. I asked her out to dinner and she said yes. Unfortunately, I had to cancel because I got a phone call to do a live stunt show for the Governor of Maryland. This woman's name was Janie. I called to cancel the date and although she couldn't believe I had done that, it worked out to my benefit a few days later.

The live stunt show for the Governor went great. Gator, I, and a couple of other stunt guys put on a great show. A couple of days later when I called Janie to apologize, she agreed to meet me for lunch in Annapolis. She pulled up in her black Jaguar. She had money. You could just tell by the way she acted, the way she dressed, the car she drove. I asked where she wanted to eat lunch. Her answer floored me.

She said, " forget lunch, let's just go to your place and have some fun."

Oh, my God, so we did just that. We made this agreement that we would just be friends and have a fun time, because she was married, though not happy, and was making plans to get a divorce (have I heard that one before).

I had established a big, bad pattern in my life, having relationships with married women, and driving fast cars, and fast boats. I had not been saved yet, had not been reborn yet. All my life I have been in search of inner peace, studying different religions, different cultures, and different beliefs. The simple answer would be God, but I didn't understand that as of yet. I was always trapped in the clutches of my addiction. Friends would always call me Crazy Mike, and in a sick way, I was proud of that. I am not so proud of that today. People still call me that at times because of what they've heard about old stories, events, or behavior that was out of the norm. You know, all my life I've had to do it my way, go it alone, and I always had to start over. I don't think everybody can do that and succeed.

Janie and I were having a wild time, just like high school kids, living life like all there would be was us and fun. I had a hard time growing up, that's basically what it came down to. I moved from job to job, partied without a care, had police troubles, and bar fights. I think back and

I feel that some of the reason for the lack of maturity was that I was trying to face the fact I had let my little girl down, I let her go. I would not ever have the chance to watch her grow up, see her graduate, see her go on her first date, or walk her down the aisle and give her away. These are pains I don't wish on anyone, I am happy she has the family that she does. I am happy that she had a father figure in her life. I hope someday, somehow my daughter gets the chance to read this. I hope she will see me again before I die.

Back to Annapolis. Janie and I started to fall in love, and that was against the original plan to just stay friends and have fun. Well, a plan like that never ever works out that way, it can't. Human beings have feelings, time would pass and I would get a job on a film in Washington, DC. It was called *The Shadow Conspiracy*. Janie came down to the set. I worked on the film for a couple of days, and then I worked on *Undefeatable,* a martial arts film that I also had a co - starring roll in. I told Janie she had to leave her husband or I was going to end our relationship and move to North Carolina. She didn't believe me, and neither did her friends. I think almost five years had gone by—we had been dating that long. I know I have left some things out, but try to stay with me. I packed up my things, I was living in a really nice townhouse on the water in Annapolis, but I left and moved to North Carolina. Janie left her husband two days after that, if you're wondering if I had trust issues with women because of the events that I allowed to happened in my life, you would be correct. I was a large man now in my adult years, five feet eight and half inches tall and normally weighing around two hundred and twenty pounds. My head was shaved but I had a pony tail in the back—a rather fashionable look, don't you think. I also carried a short men's wig in my stunt bag, just in case my look would not work for the auditions I was going on. Well, I reached North Carolina at Screen Gems Studios in Wilmington. It was under a new management team, headed up by the son of a very famous director. We would become friends. I opened an office on the studio lot and started to form a new stunt team based out of the studio. The team was called **THE ATLANTIC STUNT PLAYERS INTERNATIONAL ASSOC**. Yes, a second take of the Florida stunt team. But this team was different. There were standards they had to meet, like having a SAG card, paying monthly dues, looking for and getting work for the team. We trained a lot, put on live shows for the studio brass on occasion. I think ours was one of the first stunt teams ever located right on a studio lot. It was all good. There were times when it was tough to get work, but such is life. Janie started coming down from Maryland to visit me and we were attempting to fix things up. I have had crazy times. I have done crazy things. People have called me crazy. But I knew I was not crazy. I was dying on the inside. I was in conflict with man's world and with my God's world. I feared what I would in time know to be fact. And that fact is that I thought I should be, or wanted to be, what our society says a man at my age should be. I don't want to be anything more than who and what I am, and if someone needs to find comfort in judgment on that fact, more power to you. I had hurt people, and I'd hurt my family. I had hurt myself. I had put myself into a prison of hell between my left and right ears. I knew on my journey in life, that I would find peace someday if I lived that long, I would finally find the God of my own understanding, if I lived through this journey. I had made a lot of money and money doesn't make you happy. That is such a *bullshit* statement!

"MONEY DOESN'T MAKE THE WORLD GO AROUND"

Yes, money does make you happy; Yes, money does make your life more comfortable. It helps you get things more easily, it helps to bring security into ones life, enjoyment, to you and enjoyment to others. However, when both GOD and money are put in the proper perspective—that is when it all works.

Another one of societies bullshit lies—if money doesn't make the world go around, then you tell me why there are wars, muggings, robberies, and fraud. And why is there such a game with the court systems? And why is there organized crime? Please answer those questions for me. People who make these statements that money doesn't make you happy either never had any money, or never had enough money. If you think it sounds like I'm angry, you're right. I have come to realize, on my shift here on this planet Earth, that if people would just treat others as they wish to be treated, if they helped others in the name of God, rather than be driven just by money, we would not have the problems we have, and the world would not be in the shape it is in today.

I need to vent for a moment. Am I mad at my second ex-wife? No, Am I mad at that priest for what he did to me as a child? No, Am I mad at those cops that beat me that night in Chicago, or for what happened to me in the riot at the L.A. County jail? Or for what happened to me in my car crash? No

I'm mad at the tragic things that have happened to me because of the manner in which I was living my life, in the way that caused such defeat to myself, and the fact that I had willingly sought to cause pain and suffering to others and to myself.

The word is not "mad." The better word would be "sorry." I'm sorry those things happened. I am sorry they happened to me. I'm sorry they happened to others. I'm sorry it took me so long to look for help. I'm sorry I was afraid to tell anyone that I needed help. And I'm sorry I may never have a healthy relationship with my beautiful daughter. I am sorry we live in a world that does not understand what it means to love one another as you would want to be loved yourself. GOD in His grace and forgiveness, has let me see the error of my ways. GOD has also allowed and brought into my life the people, places, and things that have shown and taught me a NEW way to live life, A new way to treat others, My GOD has actually given me a new life.

MICHAEL WALTER's FAMOUS ONE HANDED PINKY

PUSH UP

1981

CHAPTER FIVE: BACK TO GOD

Stunt work started rolling in for the stunt team. I went back to church. I had gone to a four-day church mission where I had four days to talk with a Catholic priest. I told him what happened as a child during those four days. I came to believe that a God of my understanding could restore me to sanity. I forgave the Catholic Church, I forgave myself, I forgave that priest, I forgave those cops, my ex-wife, and I forgave God. I blamed God for what had happened to me. The sad part was, it was never God's fault. I began to release and forgive everything and everyone that in any way I felt any negative feelings about. Do I like everyone? Of course not. Can I work with everyone? Of course not. Do I wish harm on another human being that has a communication problem with me? Never, I am just trying to live my life the way I believe God wants me to live it. I pray every day my daughter has the willingness to forgive me. Do I hold myself accountable for what has happened to me in my life? One hundred percent, did you read that correctly? Yes, all that happened in my life, good or bad, was nobody's fault but mine, and I will live with that for the rest of my life. I bet you did not think this story was going to turn in this direction. It did when you first opened to page one. This is very healing for me, to finally be released from the bondage of self.

Janie and I started to patch things up, and now she was visiting every couple of months. I was drinking again, but it seemed I was controlling it. I had been living in North Carolina for three years. Now, I know I have left out all the stuff that happened in North Carolina, but such is life (smiles). Janie and I decided I would move back to Maryland and we would get back together and maybe get married. Gator was still in Annapolis.

I had introduced Gator to a very nice girl that was living in the same apartment complex. I had settled down so much. I gave the stunt team my blessings. It was 1997 and I would be competing in a national body building competition. Afterward, I moved back to Annapolis. Then I bought a place on Kent Island in the Chesapeake Bay, which is on the eastern shore of Maryland. When I moved back, Janie had met a man and had started to date him. We were done then. I still see her every couple of years and say hello. She seems so happy. You know, that's all I ever wanted for anybody, and that's all I ever wanted for her. Actually, that is all I want for myself. Now the stunt work was coming in on a regular basis. The entertainment business is a very forgiving business. These are a few films that I worked on: *Serial Mom*, *Major Payne*, *The Pelican Brief*, *Mars Attacks*, *12 Monkeys*, *The Jackal*, *This World Then The Fire Works*, *Everything's Wonderful*, and *Metro*. For the filming of *Metro*, I flew from the East coast to San Francisco to be a stunt double. The story line reads like this. I was to fight the lead actor, Eddie Murphy, in a knife fight on a busy street in San Francisco in the rain. I would double the well known actor, Mr. Paul Ben Victor. Then I would get flipped in front of a taxi cab that was moving at 20 mph and getting hit head-on. So we got ready to do the stunt. Eddie Murphy flipped me into the street. Water was pouring down from the rain machine. I stood up just as a taxi cab hit me head-on at twenty miles an hour. Don't try this at home but believe me, getting hit by a car traveling at 20 mph is very painful. The first take it hurt, but I was okay. The second take it hurt worse, and I was not okay. The third take, I broke the windshield and everybody was upset; and the fourth take—well, let's just say the fourth take did permanent damage to me. But I was working at what I loved to do. Please don't take it wrong. Every take was perfect, everybody loved them. The director wanted more angles in order to do what is called a match cut shot. That requires a lot of footage. He had that, so that would not be a problem. All he had to do to get that was two shots and slow the camera frame down. But hey, what do I know? I was just the idiot that said, "Sure! I got another one in me." I got paid a ton of money, limped back to my trailer and then went to sleep back at the hotel. I got on an airplane the next day heading back east. God, I love this business.

Moving ahead to 1999, I was definitely clean and sober now, even though I might have a beer now and then. For the most part, I had not been drinking or doing any drugs for a long time. I was going to church on a regular basis, dating, and had been working on a deal with Fox TV to do a world record fire burn, live on national TV. It took twelve months to prep for the TV show and the fire burn. It was scheduled to be held in downtown Las Vegas. The stunt got me an interview on Entertainment Tonight. This was a huge thing for me. The whole show on Fox would be about me—my career as a stuntman and the car crash. I have it on DVD today. Big deal? Yes, it was indeed. It was a great production and a great crew. All in all it turned out to be a great show except for one tiny little thing that happened.

I was having a lot of press coverage and TV interviews. I was the stunt coordinator for the show, and we had to do a practice fire burn the night before. It was a Monday night, a night that was not in the contract, but I agreed to do the extra burn, and all went great. We did all this because the producers wanted it this way. They said it was so they could be sure it would go smoothly the next day, live. My stunt team was busy the next day and night setting up for the live TV show. I forgot to have one of my stunt team members get the back-up air bottle re-filled. That was my call, and I was going to have three air bottles, but I thought because of budget we could get away with just two. And we could have, if I would have gotten the one re-filled. It seems a simple enough thing to remember, but I forgot. Anyway, I had one of the best stunt safety teams in the business working for me. I had known a few of them for many years. They were the kind of people I would trust with my life and for this stunt, I had to trust them with my life. Paula, a good friend from Pittsburg whom I had met when I worked on a film there, drove out to Las Vegas to see the fire stunt. Troy was the person who would be my second in command. When doing a stunt like this, there comes a point when you've got your wardrobe on and you're unable to communicate with the producer, cameraman, crew, and such for whatever reason. Besides, to do this stunt I had to have thirteen layers of clothing on and five hoods over my head That's why I needed a second voice.

The safety team needs a lead man, and that man was Troy. I had known him and his family for years. Like I said before, it was a big show and we were about to perform it live on national TV. So my fifteen minutes of fame were about to happen, when something went wrong with my air tank on live television. That's not cool at all. There was a lot of confusion, but the bottom line was, the one and only full air bottle my stunt team had, the one I was breathing out of, had just run out of air. An O-ring had split, and as I said before, I had not sent anybody to get the backup bottle re-filled. The TV show's producer was going to cut to a commercial, and then we would have had a couple of minutes to find a solution to our dilemma. Being the person that was in charge of this action part of the show and with time running out, I made the decision that we would go ahead with the stunt. When we came back from the commercial break, I attempted to perform this stunt. It was my 105th fire stunt in twenty years, both on film and

TV. And just for the shits and giggles for my career, I decided to do this stunt live, on national TV. I was totally engulfed in flames with the world looking on. Because there was no back-up air bottle, I performed this feat holding my breath. I stood there in my bomb zone, four propane cannons pointed at my body, waiting for the moment when the four flash pods with five, six-ounce bombs would explode. We had to make sure I was set on fire, seeing how this was a live TV production. We had no time for take two or take three or to make it work right—it had to work the first time.

I want to get off track, just for a bit. I have been working day and night on this manuscript. I had to drive over to the western shore of Annapolis today. I sold my house and will get the settlement in a couple of weeks. I had to check on some things so I stopped by a couple of clubs to say hi to some old friends. I'm telling them what I'm doing, writing this book. They all think I should have done this a long time ago. But hey, better late than never, right?

What I have come to figure out is this. I'm telling you my story, but I am attempting to write this because it might be my only way of contacting my daughter, Kyleigh. You will understand later in the book, but this whole thing is for her. And it's because of her that I've dedicated this book to her. It will be something she can have forever, sort of a journal of the father she had no clue about.

I was having a VHS tape burned to DVD disc today, so time won't destroy the TV show. When I'm old and gray, I want to look back and say, "See—I really was a Hollywood stunt man a long time ago."

Back to the story. The night of the burn went as planned. As Troy, my second in command, was preparing me to go into the bomb zone, the whole world (well at least those watching the stunt) was looking on. They saw

Troy walk me to the bomb zone and spray a lot gasoline on me to make sure I would light up.

You see, no one knew of the formulas I had invented and that I had painted all over me. Nobody really knew, including me, what the ignition point affect would be. We had seen the night before what the affect had been with propane igniting me, but we weren't certain what would happen with the full cannons, flash pods and bombs. Well, as it turned out, everybody would be in for an early Fourth of July.

The cameras were rolling for this live stunt. I said, "Action!" The special effects guy did his job and anybody that was there saw, smelled, and some felt the heat from the explosion that went off. It sent flames onto my body and into the air. I believe I was told they were thirty-two feet high. It was really an unbelievable sight to witness. I burned for one minute and fourteen-seconds, not the two minute world record which, at the time, nobody could prove even existed; it was only a rumor. But what did happen was somebody a year or so later set a real world record for two minutes and six-seconds. Still, I was proud of the fact that no stunt person has before, or since, done what I did that night. The special effects technician told the producer that when he shot the laser gun at my body, the temperature sometime after ignition was at 2500 degrees.

The producer said, "Oh my God, no! Call the hospital and we won't say that he is that hot on TV. Say something like he's over 1000 degrees." The flames were above my body about fifteen feet. So in my view, and a few others in the business, I had set two new world records. But hey, what the heck? I got paid that night. Yep, they wrote me a check. As I was getting out of wardrobe, they probably thought, "Get this guy paid before something else happens." But you know, it was a great stunt. I walked away from it safe, and everybody got paid. Nobody got hurt. I couldn't talk for a couple of months because that 2500 degree flame I swallowed dropped me like a bag of potatoes. I was not even hot but I couldn't breathe. I had tried to sneak one in the best I knew how, and whoops! It knocked the living shit out of me. So down I went, and my great stunt team put me out in record time and saved my hide again. I said, "Thanks guys, I owe you one." Troy had also been in the water tank that night in L.A. when I was drowning. Okay, Troy, I owe you two—I swear I love this business.

We all went out that night. The producers asked me to dinner, but I told them I had to take my stunt team out and that we all had early flights in the morning. I thanked them anyway. We all got a little stupid that night, but we had fun. Nobody got arrested or hurt, so it was a perfect night after all. The next morning the stunt team went back to the airport. I had some more work to finish up in the production office, and since I would be heading out in a couple of hours, we said our good-byes. They went west and I went back to the office.   Then I went back to the East coast. I have met some of the best people in the world because of this movie business. I had to get a lot of stunt gear sent back east, and then I got on my flight to head home. When I got home I thought it might be a good idea to take a long overdue rest. So I didn't work for a while. Actually, because of what happened to me with this stunt going wrong the way it did, I wanted to take some time off and re-evaluate my life. I was not a young kid anymore, and a lot of stunt people better than me had retired or had died. That was on my mind a lot, but for whatever reason, I wanted to slow down for a bit. I bought a house in the country in southern Maryland, two miles off the main road and one block away from the beautiful

Chesapeake Bay. You could see the West River out my kitchen window. There were deer, turkey and other wildlife. This is what I needed, although there was nothing to do, not any place to see movies, only a couple of restaurants. Everything was about a half hour away, malls, stores, things like that. I opened a personal training business out of my house. This was really good for me, working out and getting paid for it. I didn't have much furniture, but I did have lots of gym equipment. I had lost something inside of me, a desire. Something happened that night when the Las Vegas Fire Department and my stunt safety team saved my butt. Something happened to me inside. Maybe I was finally starting to grow up. Oh my God I think I need a drink! Just kidding

****

I was sitting in my living room the night of September 11, 2001. I know I don't have to tell you what happened that day, the day my world, like yours and many others, would change forever. I don't want to get into argument match with anybody about this subject. However, today in 2020 I'm here to tell you that this country is beginning to forget what happened that day in the year of 2001. If as a country we don't start getting a backbone and deal the way we need to deal with this kind of situation, it is going to happen to us again—it is human nature. You might disagree with me and that's your right, but I have the same rights as you, and this is how I feel about it. I saw the second plane hit the second tower on TV that day, and I just could not believe what I was seeing. I called my family, one of my sisters Karen was living in Washington, DC at that time, and has since moved. There were rumors Annapolis was a target, I had friends in New York that day. Some family was supposed to be in New York that day close to those towers, but their plans had changed. It was crazy around here, you would drive up to Annapolis, there were machine guns at the gates of the Naval Academy and federal road blocks on some streets. Washington, DC looked like a war-torn third world country. All I could think about was a twelve-year-old girl that I had not seen in ten years, and I had not a clue where she was in this world. I had no idea where her mother, my ex-wife, was living and it was driving me out of my mind. No matter what you have come to think of me and my story, after all this time, I have feelings, I wanted to know where my daughter was. I had no rights anymore because I let those rights I had as her birth parent go when I agreed to let Kyleigh be adopted. Yes, I think about that and a few other stupid decisions I have made in my life. Take it from me, when it is your child, time doesn't heal. All time does is make the pain worse every day, that I don't see her or have a chance to talk to her. I don't get to ask her how her day at school went or how cheerleading practice went. (That was a "venting" moment.)

As you all know, the USA went to war over all of that. I had a good personal training business going on at that time, a nice little house in the country near the water, and good people in my life. I was on one of my sober bouts. A year had gone by since the attack on September 11, 2001. During that year, I met a person who knew a someone that was in the business of finding people, the kind of people who really didn't want to be found. The kind of people with false phone records in someone else's name, for whatever reason, be it to elude creditors, stalkers, or ex's (husbands or wives). Anyway, I hired such a person right after September 11, 2001, to try and find my daughter. Then one day, a miracle happened. I was driving down the road on a cold snowy winter day in February 2003 I think. I got a call on my cell phone, it was that person who finds people. When I answered, the lady on the other end of the phone said, "Is this Michael Walter?" I said, "Yes it is." Then I heard, "We found them." I said, "What?" then the voice on the other end of the phone told me they had found my daughter—I almost caused a car crash. I had to pull off to the side of the road and I asked, "Where?" then the person told me where my daughter was living, and gave me her phone number. I was shocked, scared, and nervous, I really did not know what to say or do at that moment. I thanked the person on the phone and asked how much I owed, then that person said something that would have a life-long affect on me, she said, "Mike, you don't owe us a dime GOD took care of the bill" I began to weep as we ended the call.

I called the phone number that was given to me and got their answering machine. On the message was my ex-wife's voice. A voice I hadn't heard in almost ten years, I didn't leave a message; I just hung up the phone, and just sat there in my truck. I drove home and did what I always do. I worked out and trained to take my mind off what had just happened. I talk to my God, Jesus Christ. He is my friend, I'm not afraid of Him like I was as a child in Catholic school. A few days passed by, I made that phone call again, but this time someone answered the phone. It was my ex-wife's current husband. Well, I told him who I was, his response was, "What in the world do you want, and how did you get this number?"

I really couldn't blame him for his anger. He had never met me and I'm sure he only heard one side of the story, but there's two sides to every story and unless he reads this book, he won't know my side. So I left a message and my ex-wife called in a day or two after that. That was very weird, as you can imagine. Anyway, weeks went by and I was finally introduced to my daughter by phone. My heart was so filled with joy and happiness to hear her voice. I think at the time I was more nervous than she was. After that, I would talked to Kyleigh on the computer and the phone every chance I could get. A couple of months passed by when we, my daughter, ex-wife, and her husband, agreed to a visit where I could meet my daughter in person for the first time since she was two years old. It would be under supervision of course, with one or both of the parents. The first time was with my ex-wife, then with her and her husband, which was very weird. Then my ex-wife came up to Maryland with my daughter, and Terri's two sons. They stayed for part of the summer in my house. I slept outside on the patio's concrete floor, and they slept in the house—that is what we agreed to. Kyleigh made friends where I lived, and it was all going well. However, you know there was a reason why I got a divorce fifteen years prior. They went back to the South, where they lived. After that time in the story, we didn't speak for many years.

Painful, you ask? You have no idea. Every day I spent wondering, thinking about how she was, what she was doing, and wondering if she ever thought of me. There was no communication. I wrote letters, sent e-mails, but to no avail. I don't know if she ever even got them or her mom just threw them away, but I finally stopped writing.

I wrote the first edition of this book in the hope that someone who read it would know her, and tell her about it. Maybe she will hear of this book on Oprah ... who knows? As always, God put another miracle into my life, someone did read my book and shared it with her. Kyleigh did read it in her adulthood, by that time, 12 more years had passed. The next time I reached out, I did hear back from her. Before this, God had brought her into my life just three times. I never quit, never stopped, so I prayed He might do it again. I thought, even if I never saw her again, she is my little girl. When I'm gone, at least I'll have something to leave her. She will be taken care of from my retirement or insurance. See, I have done some things right. I know where she lives now, I have her phone number. She knows now, that door will always be open for her to come home if she wants.

I ran my personal training business for three years. Then I had a stunt buddy call from New York. A friend of his in L.A. called and needed some stunt men to get locked up in a maximum security prison in Maryland for a film called *XXX-2*. I felt enough time had passed since Las Vegas and I took the job. It was great, never got a film credit for it, but oh well, it happens. I've been working ever since, because this is the work I do best. I was getting older I was slowing down, then the thought came to me, maybe I would try my game in the real estate business. The market was really good at the time in Maryland, so I did just that. I got my Maryland real estate license. At first I started with a big real estate company because I liked the corporate America type of attitude, then I left and went with another large company. Only this company was a win/win situation. There was no dress code, and in the year of 2005, in my market center of Severna Park, Maryland, I became the Rookie Realtor of the Year for Keller Williams Realty.

CONCLUSION

To my daughter, Kyleigh ~ Neither one of us knows what God's plan is, but I would like you to know something from the bottom of my heart. I love you, always have. I miss you, think about you every day, the best way I can tell you what I hope, pray, and wish for is reflected in a song, courtesy of Lyric Street Records and my favorite country band, Rascal Flatt's by song writers Steve Robinson and Jeffrey Steel, "My Wish".

"I hope the days come easy and the moments pass slow and each road leads you where you want to go. And if you're faced with the choice and you have to choose, I hope you choose the one that means the most to you. And if one door opens to another door closed, I hope you keep on walking till you find the window. If it's cold outside, show the world the warmth of your smile, but more than anything, more than anything, my wish for you is that this life become's all that you want it to. Your dreams stay big, your worries stay small, you never need to carry more then you can hold. And while you're out there getting where you're getting to I hope you know somebody loves you and wants the same things too. Yeah, this is my wish —you'll never forget all the ones that love you and you'll never regret, and you help somebody every chance you get. And you find God's grace in every mistake and always give more than you take. But more than anything, this is my wish. I hope you know somebody loves you. May all your dreams stay big."

To the three females that mean the most in my life

*To my loving Mother for all she has given and done all my life. In 2006 we found out that my Mom had lung cancer. She died in my arms of complications of lung cancer on Thanksgiving night, November 23, 2006, at 8:40 p.m. To my daughter who was sixteen years old in 2006: At that time, it had been three years since I or your grandparents, aunts, and uncles had seen or spoken to you. I had seen you only three times in your whole life. Kyleigh, I will forever love you. My door will always be open and the light will always stay on. Thank you for choosing to walk back in. And to my loving wife Kelley, I feel my Mother and GOD sent you down from heaven to save my life, to show me a new way to live life. A way to help and treat people and most of all. To know how and to know when to show Love. **"ALWAYS"** All of my life,* in everything I have ever been through, the ups and the downs, there are two things that have most affected me. First, not seeing my daughter and having a healthy rela-

tionship with her for so many years of her life—now that
has changed. Second, was holding my mother and watching her take her last breath while she died in my arms.

THAT IS WHAT HURTS THE MOST

****

**

EPILOGUE:

On June 27, 2007, I arrived in Albuquerque, New Mexico
to start a new life and to love again.

ROAD TO REDEMPTION

June 27, 2007 – 2020 Albuquerque New Mexico

Well, I am sure you thought that would be the end of
the story. But oh no this is now the third edition and it in-
cludes this latest information.

After my mom died, I was very much confused and
messed up inside, not sure where to go or what to do. I
moved to my uncle's house in Fairfax, Virginia and started
to work for the Lowe's Home Improvement Center in their
plumbing department. Doing this left one of my sisters in
a big jam, because we had bought a house together in
Ridgely, Maryland. I worked for Lowe's for about six
months and once again I was getting that restlessness in
my blood. I had decided to move back out west. I guess I
was thinking I could start my stunt career again in California. My book, the first edition had just been published—that's right, the first edition of this book. I didn't
have it edited or the typos corrected because I just wanted it out; I didn't care. But now almost thirteen years have

gone by, I am more settled in my mind, my life, and I do care. I care about a lot of things, one of which is to finish this book in the proper way for both you and me. I have always believed in God, but I don't think I had a true personal relationship with Jesus Christ as I do now. Now a lot of what will be said in this chapter will be about my new association with my God.

I transferred with Lowe's to Albuquerque, New Mexico, the store on the West side of the city. I arrived on June 27, 2007. Not much water out in New Mexico, but what a beautiful place. I guess I always thought of this place as sand and desert, by no means is it just that. New Mexico is full of mountains, trees and snow in the winter time. I had to get a hotel room for about a week until my apartment was ready. See, I actually planned this trip. For the first time in my life, I saved some money and planned what I was going to do. At first thought, I was headed back to L.A. back to Hollywood to re-kick start my movie career. At least that's what I thought I was doing, God had other plans. There is a funny saying someone told me once, "If you want to make God laugh, tell Him your plans." And boy was I in for a huge surprise!

I was working at Lowe's for a few months, got promoted to plumbing department Manager. I wasn't happy there, I was not happy where I was living. So I quit my good-paying job, broke the lease at my apartment, and moved to a nice part of town called the North East Heights, right at the base of the Sandia Mountains. Sandia is the Spanish word for watermelon. The mountains have this name because they look pink, like the inside of a watermelon, at sunset.

Old friends started hearing I was back and working now and then. I stayed at a very nice apartment for six months, and then right before my lease was up, a couple of things happened. My cell phone was shut off, as was the gas to my apartment. I hadn't worked consistently, in a while and wasn't able to pay those bills. Once again, I was at a turning point in my life. I had made a friend and we started going to church. She was just a good friend and that's what I needed then. Well, I had to make up my mind, was I going to stick this out or run again? My normal behavior is fight or flight, but who was I fighting? I was fighting myself.

There were no more excuses, no one to blame, I had gotten myself into this, and I was going to get myself out of it. I bought a tent and moved up to the East Mountains and lived in the woods for five months. During this time a friend from high school read a note on a message board that I had put up years ago. Remember my high school love Margie in Chapter 1? The note read that if anybody knew where Margie was, would they please contact me.

Well, sure enough, after 35 years I would finally find out what happened to Margie. What's more, I would be able to write, e-mail, and talk to her. I even came close to seeing her in person. It was almost surreal when we first started talking again. There were so many memories and stories, things about both our pasts, our families and each of our own lives, about both of our struggles with family and friends—it was heartwarming. She allowed me to cry, to tell her how much I loved her back in high school, and how sorry I was for walking out on her. You see, I was one messed up dude, I guess. For all those years I was throwing myself a pity party about how she walked out on me. That made it easy for me to blame her for how troubled my life was. But you must understand, the only reason my life was screwed up in the first place was because of me and how I did or didn't handle the events I had caused in my life. It was my fault, and only mine, not Margie's not

Joanne's, not my Dad's, not jail, not drugs, and not my mom's death.

Well, Margie and I talked and we still talk today. She always was, and still is, a great friend. At first I wanted to see her again, you know, to see if there was anything left after 35 years. Thank God there is something left between us, and that is a great understanding and deep friendship, the type of friendship where either one of us could call the other if we needed to and just talk. She helped me to let go, she helped me move on. She helped me find love again, but not with her. With the woman I would be getting married too.

You see God had forgiven me a long time ago. He had forgiven me of my sins, for now, and forever, and I had no clue at the time what that even meant. You have gotten to know a great deal of my life: my struggles, my triumphs, my victories, and most assuredly you have known my defeats, but more importantly— all the many changes in my life.

Together we have walked in and through my life's journey. Maybe at some point in my story, you cheered me on; maybe at other times you said to yourself, "He got what he deserved." In either case, you were correct. You see, this story is a very sad story, and we all have them. This story tells of one man's struggles in his life, of his losses, his victories, his great stories, his wonderful family and friends, those that have gone, those that are still in his life, and those he has yet to meet. As I look back on my life, I can't help but smile and sometimes even laugh. Wow, what a life I've had. What wild and wonderful times we shared. Yes, I am including you in this because you were there with me, through it all. Okay, maybe you weren't there in real time, but you were there in this time, in the here and now as I wrote and re-wrote this book. In many ways it is sort of sad, for this is the last chapter of this book, but not the end of the story.

It's not the end by far, not even close. This *is* the end of a very sad story and the beginning of a better one. A few years back, a funny thing happened, I put a call in to Margie and left a message. She called me back, and we talked about life, as we do when we talk now. She told me about her boyfriend and her kids from when she was married before. I told her about my Kelley, whom I have not yet told you about, and how we have spoken via e-mail a couple of times, a woman I've had a chance to talk to, but not extensively. I didn't go into detail with her about Kyleigh, as you will soon come to realize. Okay, so I lived in a tent for five months up in the East Mountains in the woods with bears, mountain lions, a hot tub and pool...... yes, it was rough. It was a very nice RV Park, but still I was in a tent in the woods. It snowed once. It was a trip, but my point is this, I was not going to quit going after my dream, no matter what. So, in the woods with my laptop, computer, and my printer, I started Albuquerque Stunt Association, LLC. Once I moved back into town, I trained stunt players there for about five years. You know it has been worth it all, really. Work has been a little slow because of the possible Screen Actors Guild strike. I am still working, but I need to tell you a great, maybe the best love story ever told. One day, actually it was October 21, 2008, I was going to my post office box to pick up the office mail. The PO Box is on the other side of town. When I pulled in to the post office, the view of the snow capped mountains was just breath taking. It was your normally sunny, beautiful New Mexico day. There was nothing out of the norm, nothing to sense this day might be the day that would change my life forever (again). I know what you're thinking, but please just follow me. I walked into the post office, down to where my PO Box was located.

The place was very busy as usual, Nothing seemed out of place. It wasn't that I thought my life was in danger, nothing like that at all. I turned left

and walked a bit, then turned to the right, stopped and took my keys out to open the box. I took out my mail, then closed and locked the box, as I turned around a miracle happened.

Out of nowhere, God and my mother sent me an angel. This tall, long-legged blonde was standing there, reading her mail. She looked up and our eyes met. I said, "hello" and she said ."hello" back. She was holding a Muscle and

Fitness magazine. She said to me, "I don't know why I get these would you like to have it?" Like the song says, she had me from hello. We talked for a few minutes and I

asked if I could give her my business card. She was kind and said sure, she picked up her mail and started to exit the building. I said, "It was nice to meet you, God Bless." She smiled and just nodded, as she turned to walk away I asked her if she would e-mail me. She turned her head back to look at me and said, "Probably not," and walked away.

Note:

The main reason I needed to write a few new pages, is that in the first edition, my story just ended with no hope, no happy ending. It just was a sad story that happens to a lot of men growing up. However, I am not just another sad story. No, my story is one of hope, courage, determination, and the belief that with God, all things are possible. Just look where I came from, what I put myself through! More importantly, please listen to where I am headed.

I believe it all comes down to this. We all have opportunities and make choices in life. I diluted my sane thinking into insane acts of bizarre, sometimes criminal behavior. Why? Who knows? Maybe someday science will be able to find an answer to this, but it hasn't happen yet. It is what it is, I did what I did, and I ask God for forgiveness for both my actions in those matters, and the actions of others that I chose to allow into my life. You may agree or you may disagree with my viewpoint. If you disagree, I would like to challenge you, but not to fight with me. Rather, walk with me, pick up a Bible, and read it all the way through. And after you have read the entire Bible, I would like to sit down with you and discuss the book of Revelations and then ask you what is it exactly you are disagreeing with me on.

I hope, as I fulfill my quest to complete this book in its proper form, and as I further my acting and voice over career, you might understand this. You know, as I come to the close of this short, but most important chapter of this book—it brings to mind the state of our nation and world affairs. We live in a very challenging time. There have been wars, our economy has more or less collapsed, we seem to be on the brink of global change, and COVID -19 has stopped the world. Why is it so hard to hear, to see, and to understand that it is our choices that have caused this entire calamity to occur? It is our separation from God that is causing the events that are happening now.

This is only one man's simple opinion, but this man has been through hell and back, both of which were my own choices. May I leave you on the subject of God with this last saying? There is a God, whatever you may conceive Him to be and I will respect that but please, from the bottom of my heart may you seek peace and strive to be happy. May God bless you and your families.

Well, weeks passed and I never heard from that lady I had met in the post office. But I just knew that God and my mom sent her to me. I believed that deep in my heart and I trust my feelings today. They guide me in most of what I do and what I say, but you know sometimes, NO all the time, God's plan works out a lot better than my own.

My first date with Kelley was on November 9, 2008. As I was writing this chapter, we had been dating for six months. In every way this is the healthiest most loving and caring, fun, thought provoking relationship I have ever had in my life. Kelley that long-legged blonde at the post office, did finally e-mail me. It would not have happened if Kelley's best friend, Sandra hadn't encouraged her to e-mail me. Kelley thought it might not be a good idea, but Sandra said, "What the heck—go out and have some fun! *Y-not?*" Now you can't pull us apart. We walk, bike, rollerblade—well, she rollerblades, I bike. We shoot guns together at the range. We go to movies, stay home, have cook-outs, and go to church, sometimes twice a week. I talk to God every chance I can.

"To get something you never had, you have to do something you never did."   When God takes something from your grasp, He's not punishing you but merely opening your hands and heart to receive something better. Concentrate on this sentence,

"The will of God will never take you where the grace of God will not protect you."

I started voice over work professionally. You see, people can, and do, change, but they have to want to change. Dreams can and do come true. Aim high, don't give up. Your dreams and desires were placed there by God. Do I walk with a halo over my head? Not at all, if I ever have a halo on, most of the time it is wrapped around my neck (smile).

In closing, I want to thank you, my family, and my friends. Yes, I want to thank you all. Because all of you have helped me in my journey, I have felt something as I have re-written this book. It's a feeling of completion, not an ending, but more of a life-changing event. I feel deeply that we all have connected in some special way. Maybe you understand what I am attempting to express to you in these final pages and maybe you don't. I understand, and that's what I am thanking you all for. If I had to do it all

over again, would I change anything? No, because everything happens in God's time, not mine.

Everything that I have allowed to occur, for whatever reason, it had to happen the exact way all the events happened. Is there sadness, sure; do I wish my behavior would have been different, sure; but it is what it is, and it has made me the man I am today. Life is a wonderful thing, I only wish I would have understood that a long time ago.

One thing my mother said to all of us before she died, "Please love and take care of each other". So I'd like to leave that gift to you all.

THE WALTER FAMILY

Maybe, just maybe, we may meet somewhere, some place, on my road to redemption.

NOT THE END—IT'S THE BEGINNING

The year is 2020, and so much has happened. I pulled the first and second editions of this book out of print then changed the titled so it would match the screenplay. The new title of both book and the screenplay are 'Face the Fire". There is so much to tell and I promise this will be the end of this book. Ok lets start were we left of, remember Kelley the tall blonde who I met at the post office, well we dated for five years and moved in together. Then on April 4, 2014, we got married, and as I said in my wedding vows Kelley saved my life. It was a great and beautiful wedding. Some of my family, my brother Rick, and sister Donna, flew out from the East coast to be there, and of course Kelley's family and friends from New Mexico came. We had it web-casted all over the place, Hawaii included. My older sister Karen was viewing it from her hospital room back east, it was a wonderful time. Sadly, she would pass away a month later from cancer. Kelley and I would spend a two week vacation, on the islands of Hawaii. One week on a boat cruise around all the islands, and the second week we had an oceanfront home on the North shore of Oahu. Memories to last a lifetime.

History Lesson: Originally a"rather tough beer bar," the Palomino was leased in 1952 by Bill and Tom Thomas of Indiana, who later bought the club, located at 6907 Lankershim Boulevard. It became popular in 1959 when the major country music showcase Riverside Rancho in the Silver Lake neighborhood shut down, leaving the various performers it had hosted available for the Palomino. In the early 1970s, the club could seat 400 attendees. [1] The Palomino Club was notable because in addition to being the San Fernando Valley's premiere night club, it was a neighborhood working class bar (opening at 6am with a happy hour from 8am to 10am)! The Palomino Club bar

stayed open during afternoon sound checks so regular customers and the artists' fans could see the bands preparing and rehearsing the evening's show for free. Often the artists' showed appreciation for the fans by performing impromptu mini-concerts to standing ovations. The Palomino's dressing rooms and backstage areas were generally open to the public. Fans could ask if the Artists were receiving visitors and most artists welcomed them, gladly signing autographs, etc. During the '50s and '60s, almost every notable country and western artist played there, but in the early '70s, The Palomino started letting the longhaired rock 'n' rollers on stage. In the '80s, The Palomino Club was home to the "Cow Punk" variety of country rock, breaking in acts like Rosie Flores, Lone Justice and The Long Riders. Many famous artists like The Flying Burrito Brothers and Dwight Yoakam played early dates there as warm-up acts. Emmylou Harris and her Hot Band regularly sold out the house. Special event concerts by musical giants like Elvis Costello, and   Neil Young created sensational disturbances in the neighborhood.

With huge crowds outside and resulting media attention. Special unannounced guests routinely joined artists onstage for

duets or jam sessions. One amazing night George Harrison, John Fogerty and Bob Dylan joined Jesse Ed Davis and Taj Mahal onstage for an improvised mini-set of some of their hits. After the death of both original owners

Billy and Tommy Thomas, the club struggled, but could not maintain the earlier momentum as it became economically difficult to attract the high caliber acts in such a small venue. The Palomino Club was a unique venue the likes of which will never be seen again. The club closed in 1995

MICHAEL AND KELLEY WALTER

2020

There is nothing stronger
than a broken man who has
rebuilt himself.

KELLEY AND MICHAEL WERE MARRIED ON 4/4/14 @ 4:00pm

NATIONAL ENQUIRER ARTICLE

A MAN CAN FAIL MANY TIMES, BUT
HE IS NOT A FAILURE UNTIL HE GIVES
UP

IN SUMMARY

As you can imagine by now a lot has changed in the world and in my life and the lives of my family and friends. What I have learned in my journey is how wonderful life is and how in most cases, people in general are good. My walk with God has definitely had it's ups and downs. My personal struggles have been and continues to be an everyday challenge. I still battle with how to deal and communicate with people, to verbally share my true thoughts and feelings. Because of my past and violent behavior in dealing with stressful situations, I am now attempting to do studies and research on the subject of body language and personality disorders in the human race. My old ways didn't workout real well as you know. But all in all I am, for the most part, doing great with it. My life and all the gifts in it are truly a blessing from GOD. My wife Kelley, my two step daughter's Lauren and her boyfriend Sam, Anie and her husband Ethan, my daughter Kyleigh, and her husband Chad, and our grandchildren Asher, Aria, and Leon. You see Kyleigh and her family did come back into my life, our lives, and the families are growing—Simply put, miracles my friend, miracles…All of them have shown and taught me, in their own special way, about life, how to live it in a more peaceful, and mindful way. And let's not forget retirement.Oh my GOD, I retired from Stunt work when I was 62, and in November 2020 I will be 67 years old—I just love it. Kelley retired in July 2020. I still work in the entertainment industry, but just when I want to, as an Actor and Voice Over Talent. I have re-written this book, and a movie deal from this book is in future plans. (same title) I am happy, healthy, and I have the best family. I have paid my dues in society, I am a productive citizen, GOD has forgiven me. I am a very blessed man. Some people say I am a lucky man. Disagree, lucky men win little things in life, or find little things, you see I am a blessed man because I found, love, I found happiness and I found my true self. Most importantly, I found and have a relationship with Jesus Christ my Lord and Savior and because of Him and for that reason.

I WON!!!

1980

2016

FROM KYLEIGH

ALBUQUERQUE, NEW MEXICO

NEVER STOP DREAMING

MICHAEL WALTER -

1976

SIFU DANNY INOSANTO and MICHAEL WALTER

GUESS WHO

1976

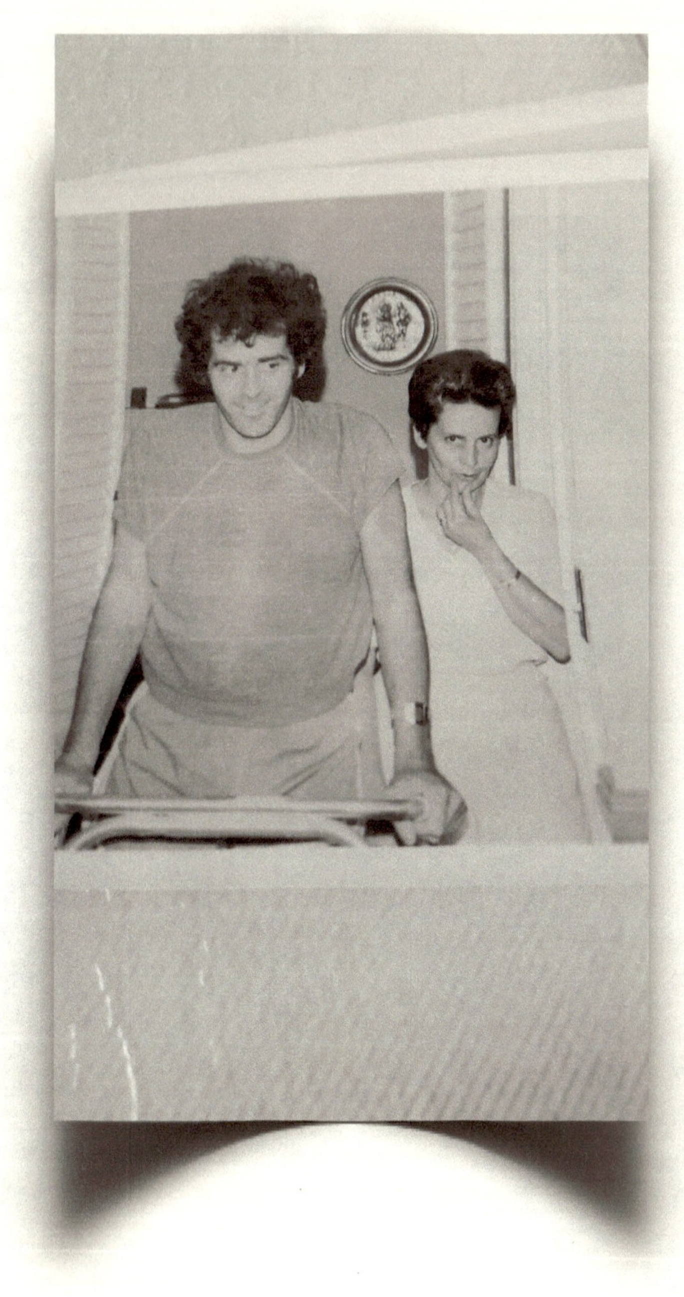

MICHAEL AND HIS MOTHER

1980

STUNTMAN JOHNNY BECKER AND MICHAEL WALTER ON STUNT JOB

IN BALTIMORE MARYLAND - 2005

AT SAINT SIMONS ISLAND, GEORGIA - 2018

FILM DEMON WIND

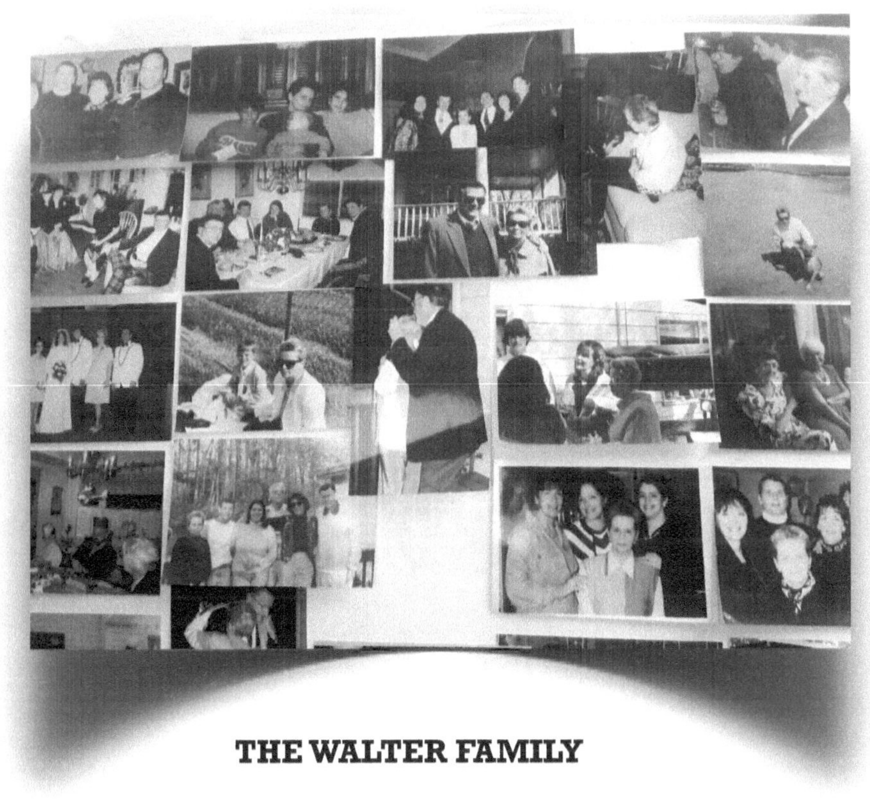

THE WALTER FAMILY

TYBEE ISLAND, GEORGIA

MICHAEL AND HIS TWO YEAR OLD DAUGHTER KYLEIGH

MICHAEL WALTER - 2020

MICHAEL S. WALTER

MY VERY FIRST HEADSHOT - 1983

JKD and KALI DEMO TEAM - 1981

SEASON FINALE OF THE TV SERIES BREAKING BAD

DAR ROBINSON (LEFT PICTURE)

THANKS FOR GOING ON THIS JOURNEY WITH ME THROUGH ALL THE MANY CHANGES IN MY LIFE. MAY GOD BLESS YOU ALL, AND MAY ALL YOUR DREAMS COME TRUE. THEY ARE A TRUE GIFT FROM GOD AND ALWAYS REMEMBER;

" TO LOVE AND TAKE CARE OF EACH OTHER"

TEN GALLON WATER BOTTLE STRETCH

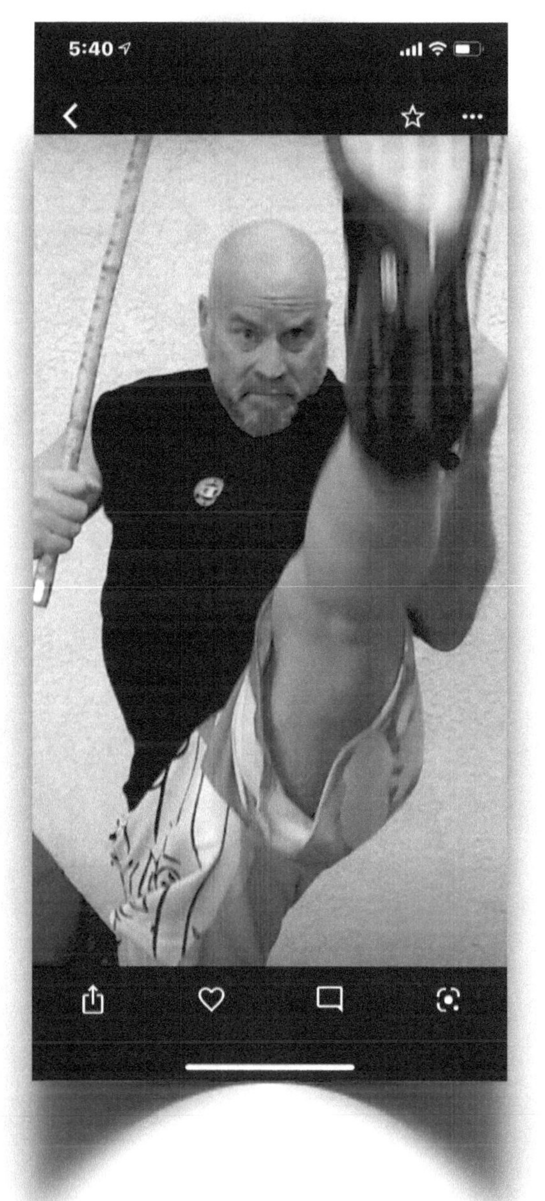

MICHEAL WALTER, FRONT SNAP KICK

AT 66 YEARS OLD

MICHAEL AND KYLEIGH

I DO WANT YOU ALL TO KNOW,

THROUGH ALL THE CHANGES IN

*MY LIFE, I REALLY HAVE NO REGRETS, IT MADE ME
INTO THE MAN I AM TODAY, MAY YOU ALL BE BLESSED*

A MRICLE

THANK YOU GOD

Always remember, Love and take care of   each other.

www.ingramcontent.com/pod-product-compliance
Lightning Source LLC
Chambersburg PA
CBHW031312160726

47993CB00001B/384